UNITED KINGDOM TOWN PLANS

3 Northern England including Scotland and Northern Ireland

J. M. Longbridge

Oct. 5th 1981

Lou

RAC UNITED KINGDOM
TOWN PLANS

3 Northern England
including
Scotland and
Northern Ireland

Containing 108 plans

Published by
THE ROYAL AUTOMOBILE CLUB
83–85 Pall Mall
London SW1Y 5HW

First published 1978
Second impression 1979

Cartography and town plan design
by the Royal Automobile Club Touring Services,
based on Ordnance Survey with the sanction of
The Controller, HM Stationery Office.
Crown copyright reserved.

© The Royal Automobile Club 1978

ISBN 0 902628 51 8

Book designed by Derek Morrison

Prepared and printed by photolitho by
BAS Printers Limited
Over Wallop, Hampshire
and bound by
William Brendon and Son Limited
Tiptree, Colchester, Essex

MADE AND PRINTED IN GREAT BRITAIN

Index to Town Plans

SPECIAL NOTE: The town plan section in *Book I Southern England* comprises pages 8–64 and the numbering of the town plan sections in Books 2 and 3 begins on pages 65 and 129 respectively.

UNITED KINGDOM TOWN PLANS

Most motorists are familiar with the use of an atlas as an aid to route planning. Most are able to translate atlas and map features into reasonable navigation when driving on Britain's motorways and road system.

But when it comes to finding their way through a medium-sized town they may be daunted by the mix of no entry and one-way signs, and the many other instructions to drivers—all of which tend to create a generally confusing pattern. This is where *RAC UK Town Plans* will prove ideal companions.

They have been designed essentially as a motorist's guide to towns. They are made up of plans which are as up to date as possible at the time of going to press. Each plan shows the Club's recommended routes through the towns and included are the various parking facilities and one-way street systems for motorists entering congested areas. For some of the larger towns a detailed companion plan indicates by-pass roads which may be used to avoid the town centre.

Some idea of the further usefulness of the guides may be gained from the fact that many of the plans contain such information as the position of public buildings and places of interest, municipal buildings, hospitals, tourist information centres, football grounds, post offices, churches, police stations, public conveniences, bus and railway stations, aerodromes, pedestrian precincts and RAC area offices.

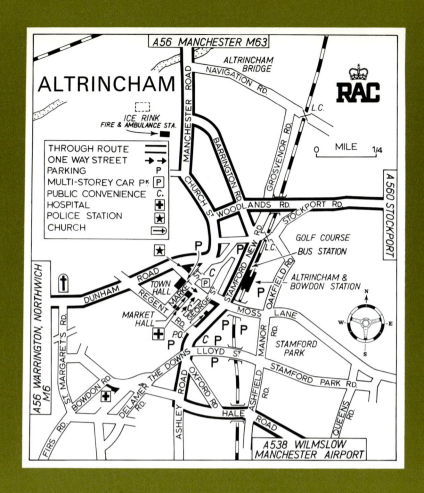

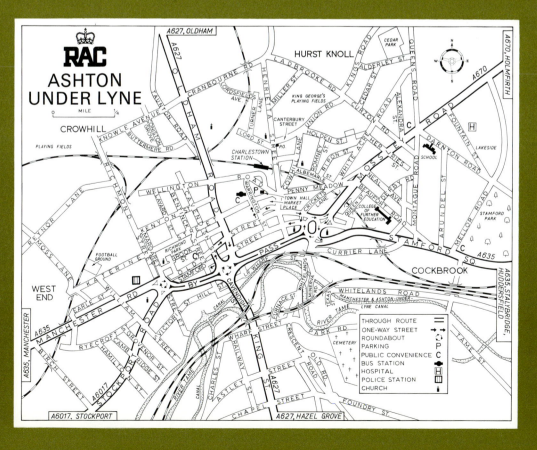

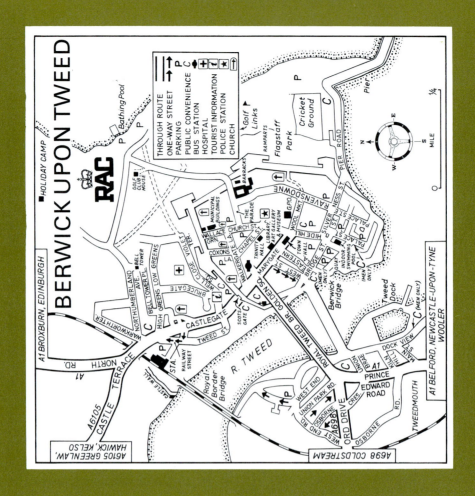

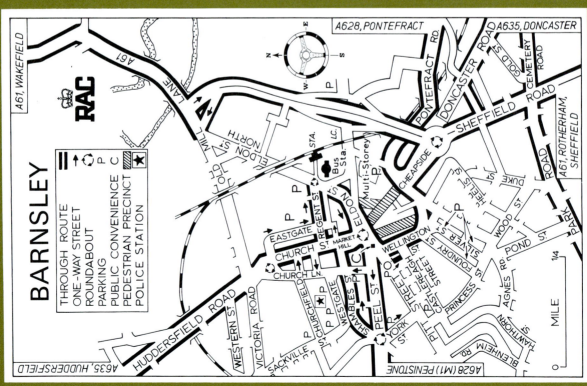

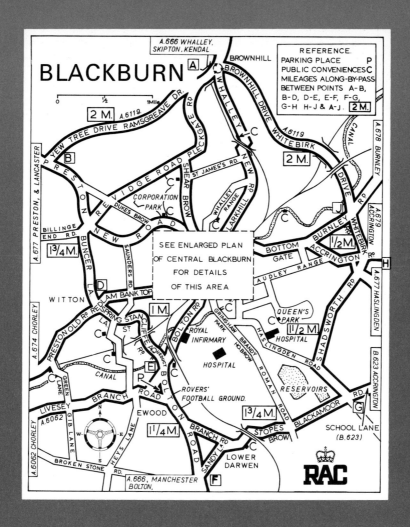

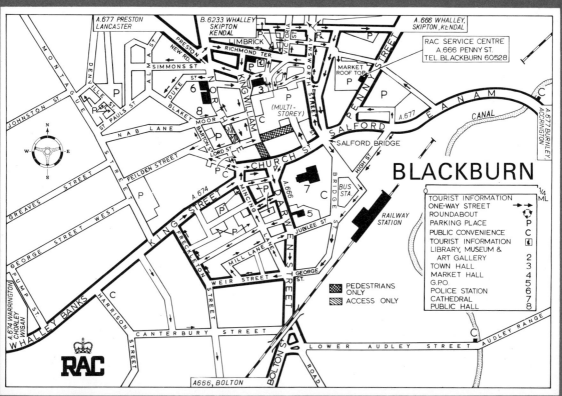

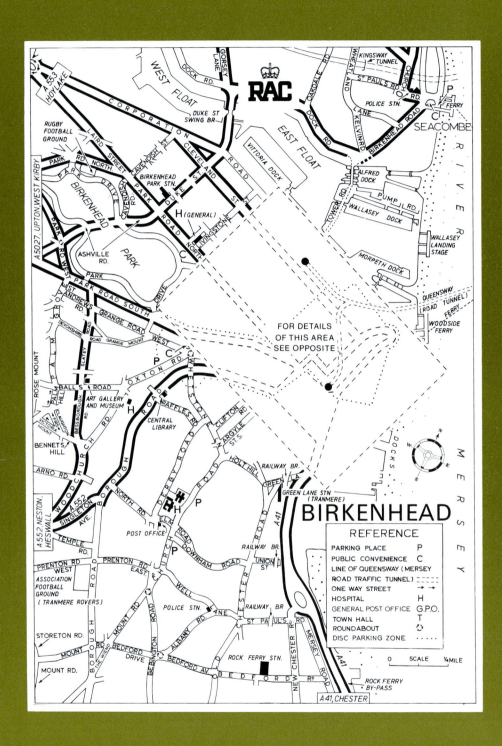

RAC

BIRKENHEAD

REFERENCE

PARKING PLACE	P
PUBLIC CONVENIENCE	C
LINE OF QUEENSWAY (MERSEY ROAD TRAFFIC TUNNEL)	- - - - -
ONE WAY STREET	→
HOSPITAL	H
GENERAL POST OFFICE	G.P.O.
TOWN HALL	T
ROUNDABOUT	↻
DISC PARKING ZONE	· · · · ·

FOR DETAILS OF THIS AREA SEE OPPOSITE

0   SCALE   ¼ MILE

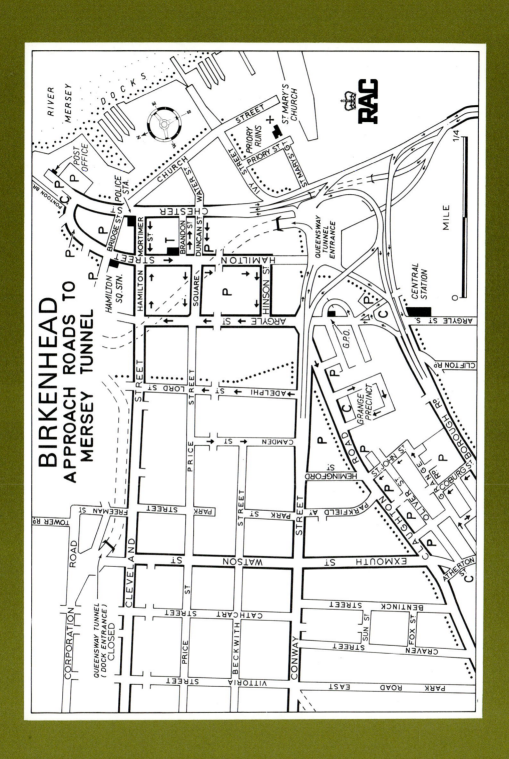

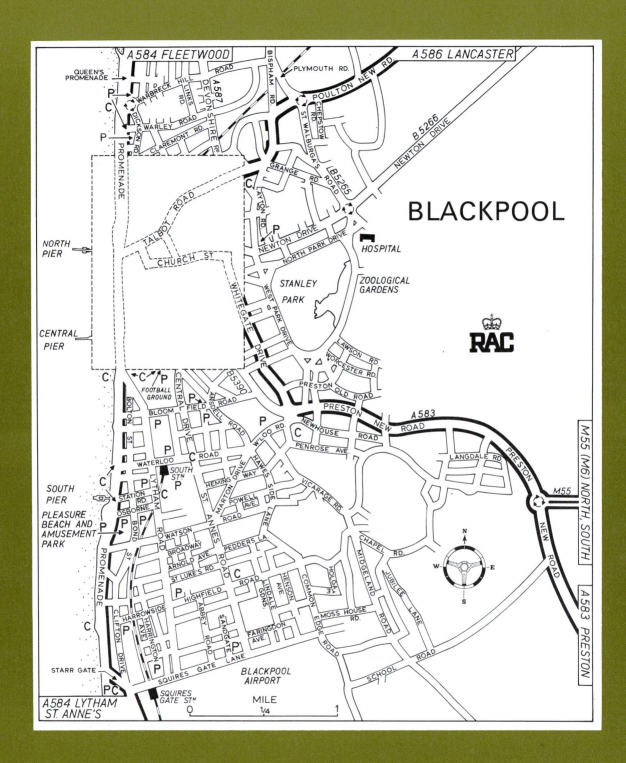

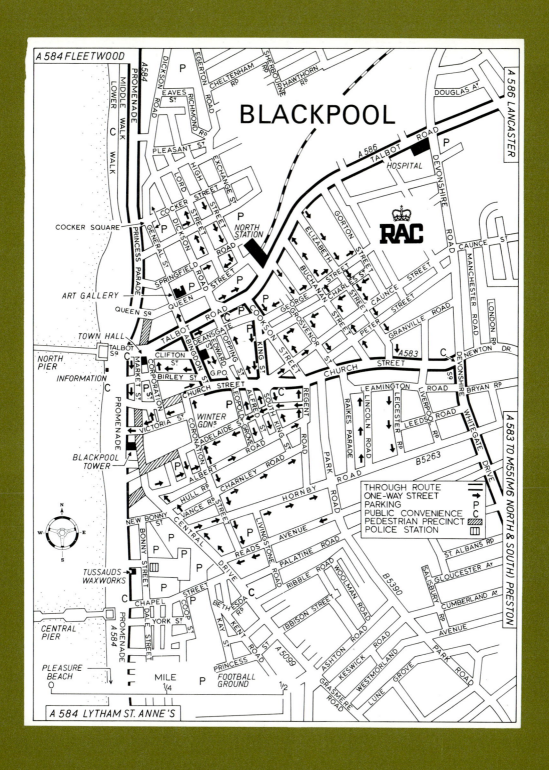

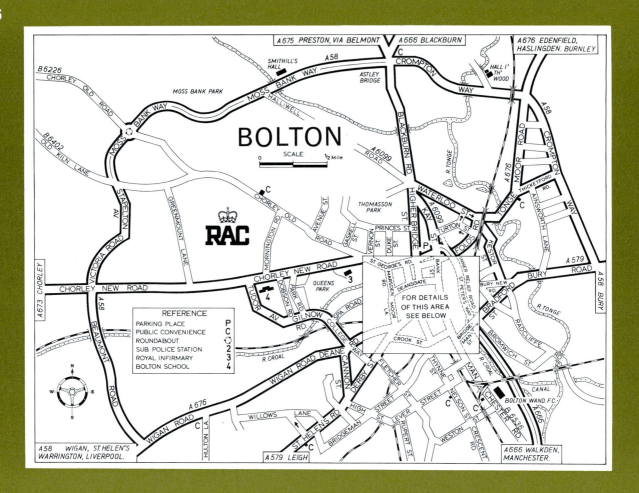

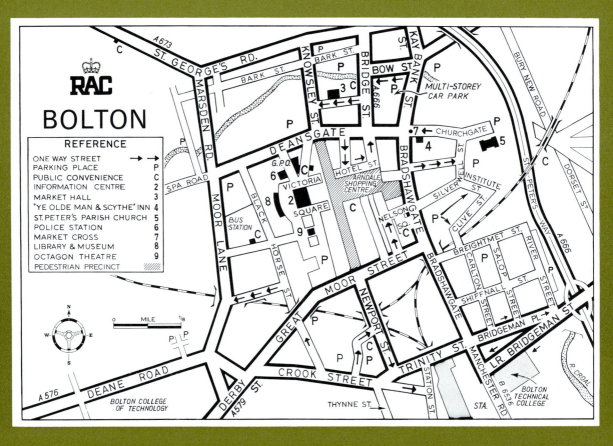

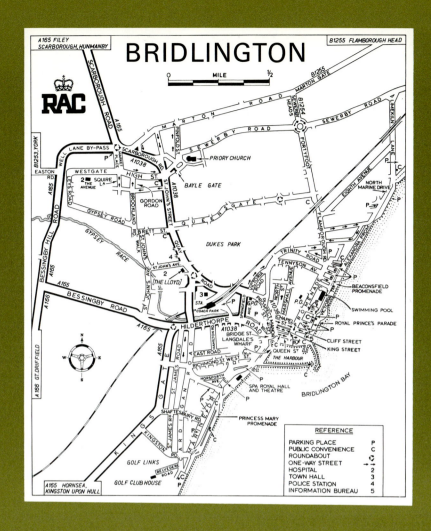

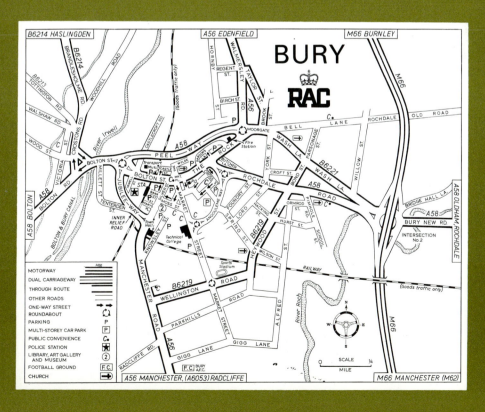

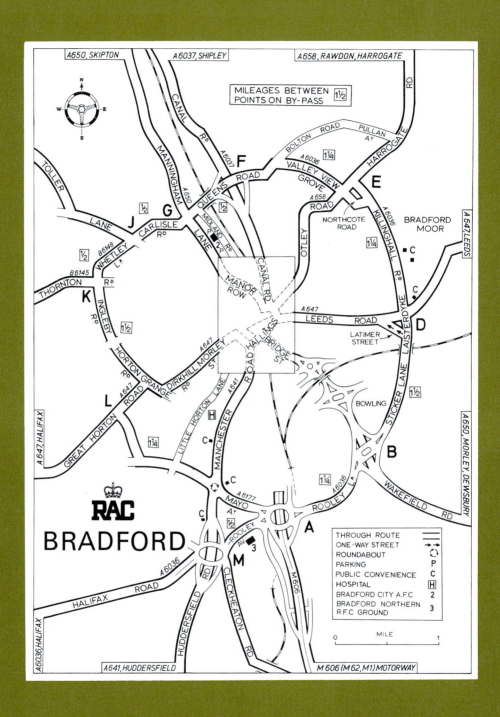

RAC

BRADFORD

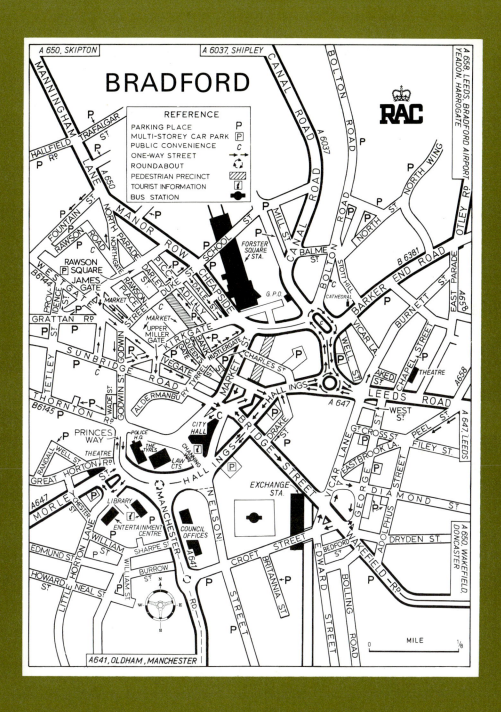

BRADFORD

REFERENCE

PARKING PLACE	P
MULTI-STOREY CAR PARK	P
PUBLIC CONVENIENCE	C
ONE-WAY STREET	→
ROUNDABOUT	
PEDESTRIAN PRECINCT	
TOURIST INFORMATION	i
BUS STATION	

RAC

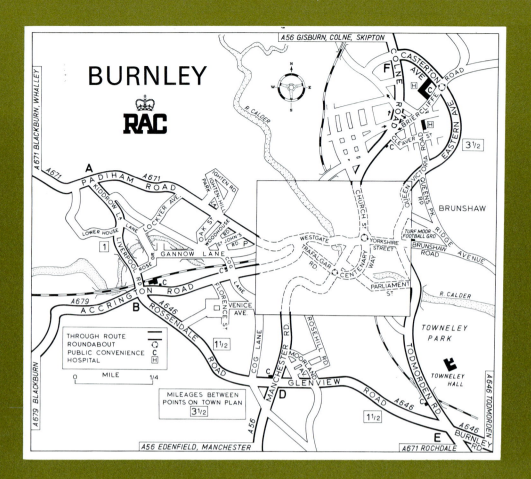

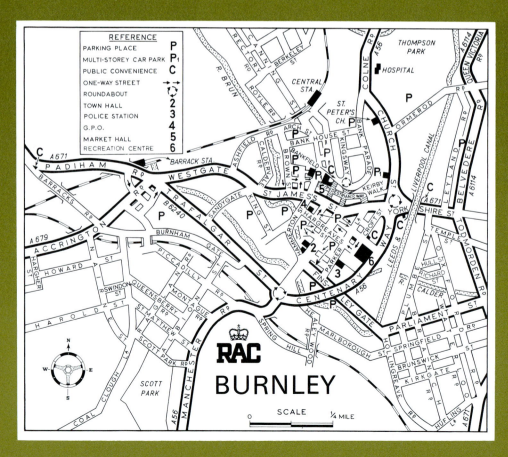

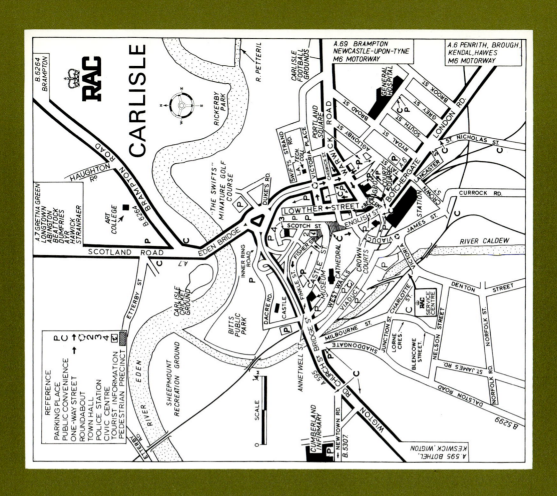

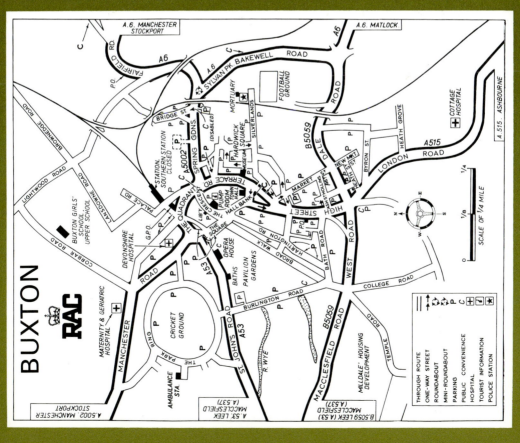

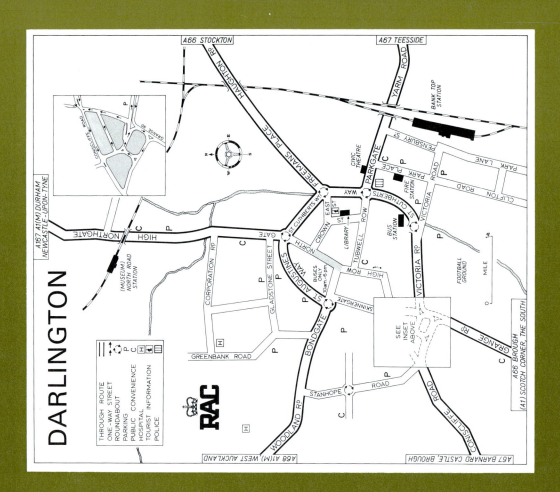

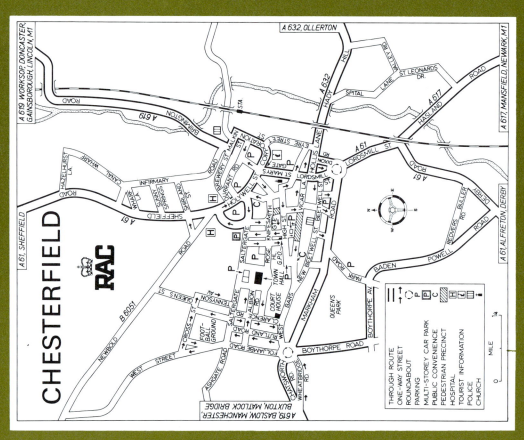

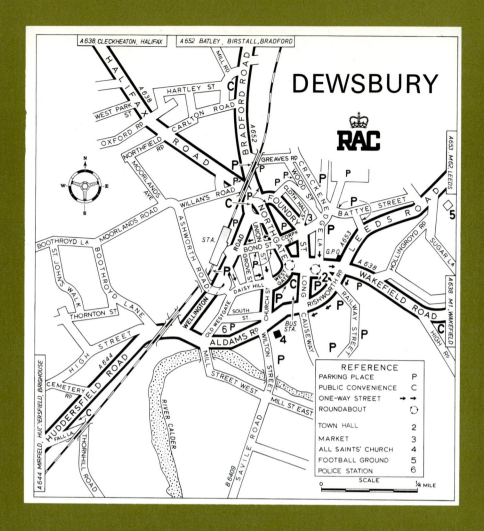

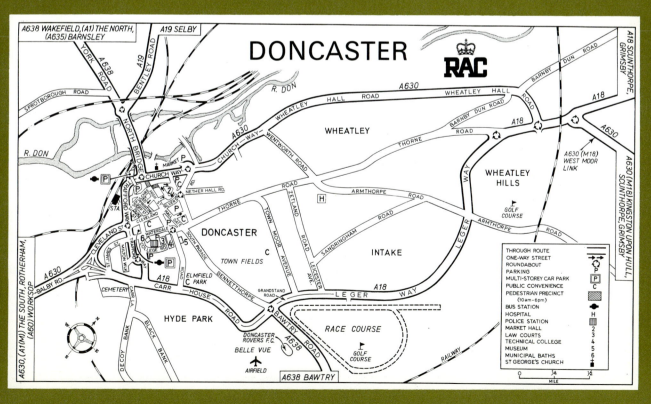

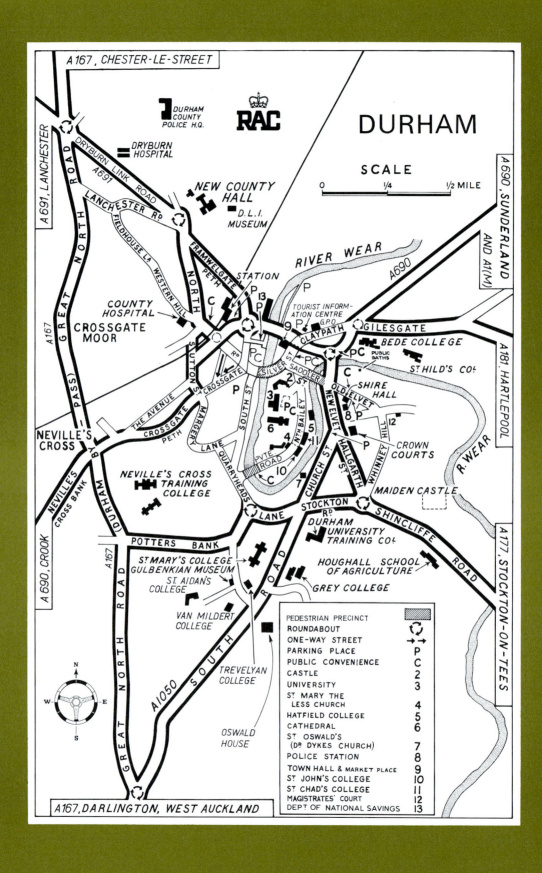

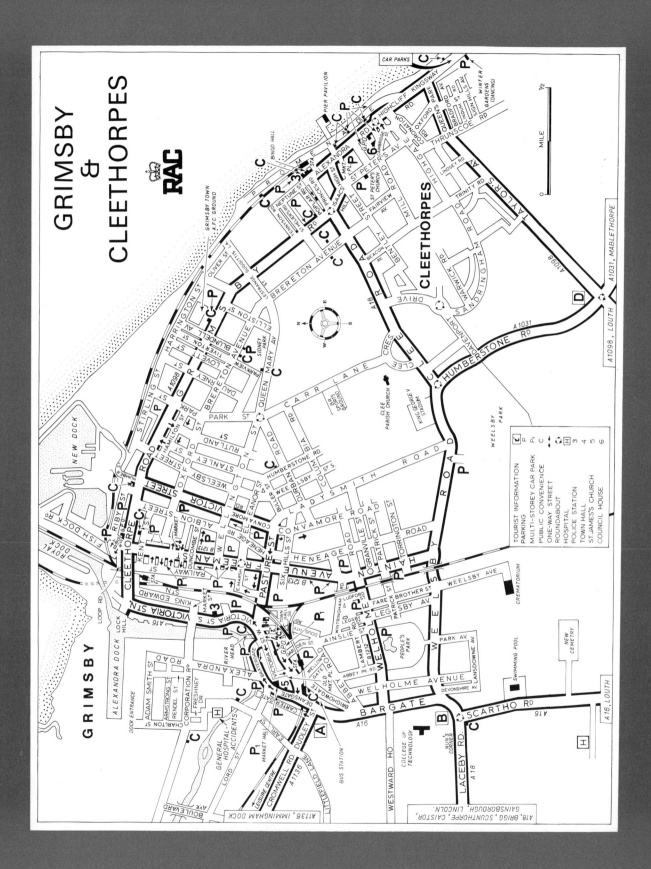

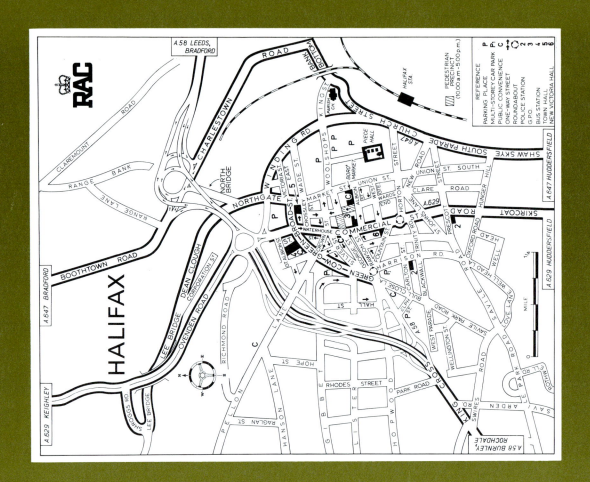

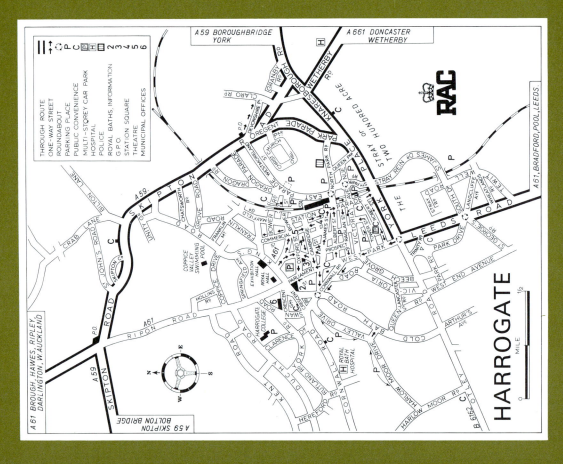

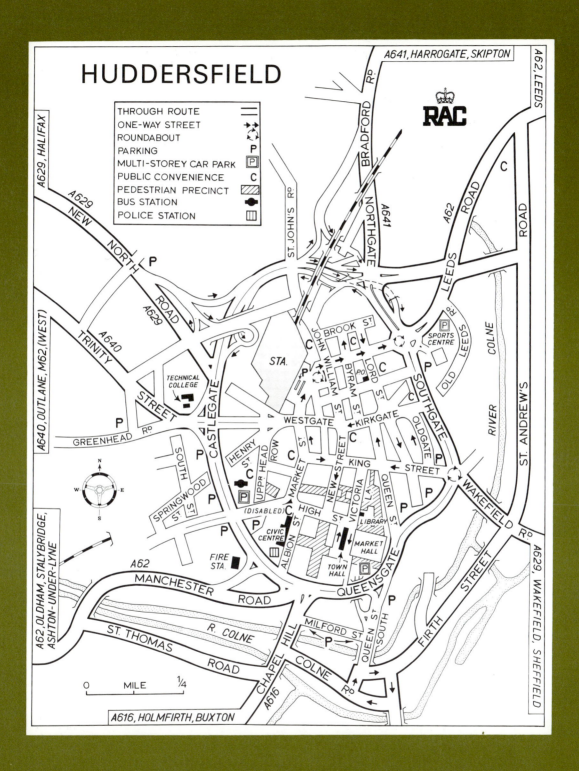

HUDDERSFIELD

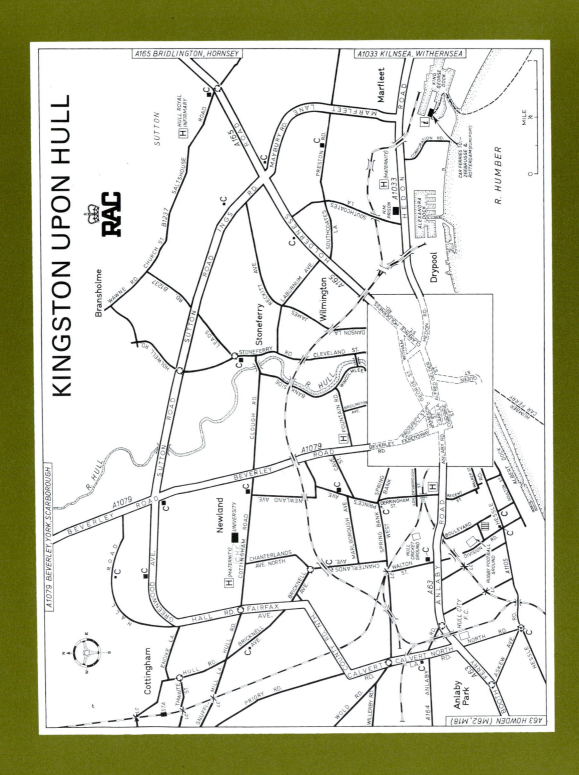

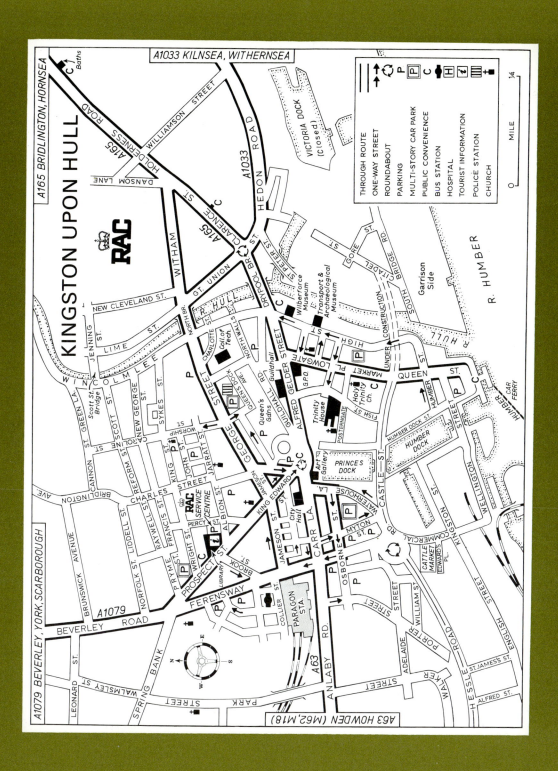

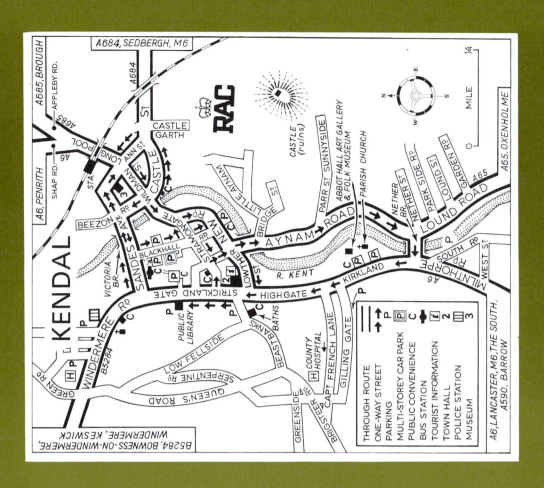

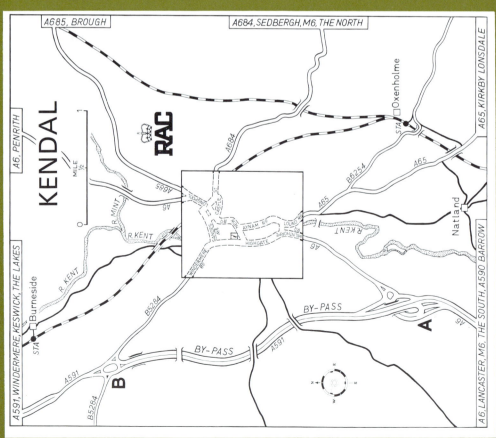

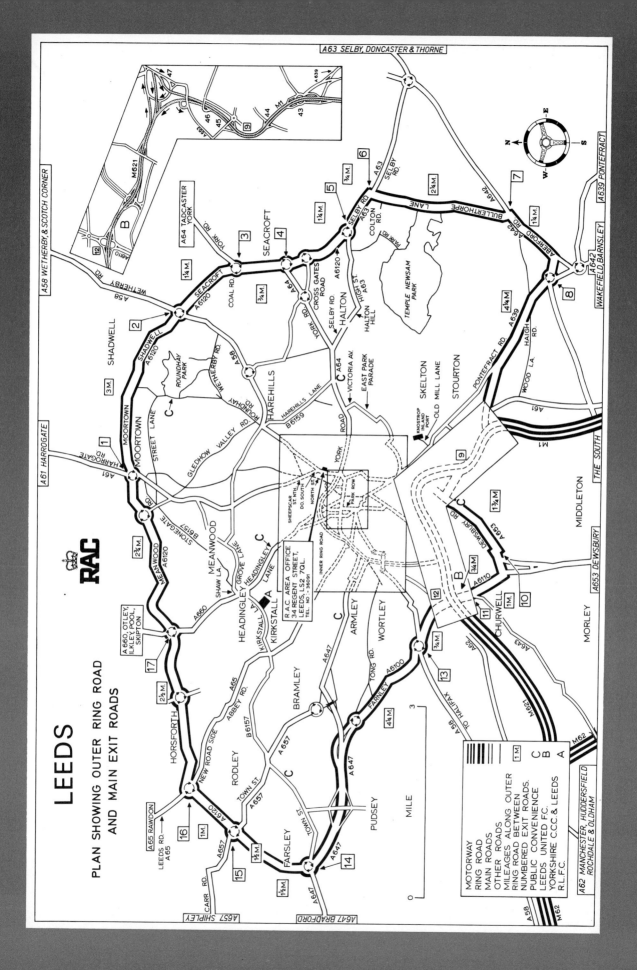

LEEDS

PLAN SHOWING OUTER RING ROAD AND MAIN EXIT ROADS

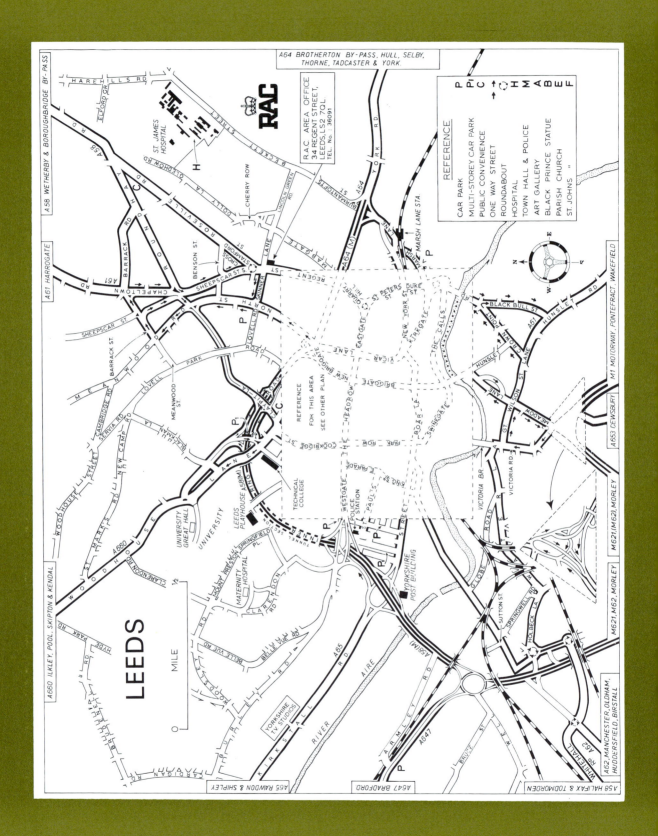

LEEDS

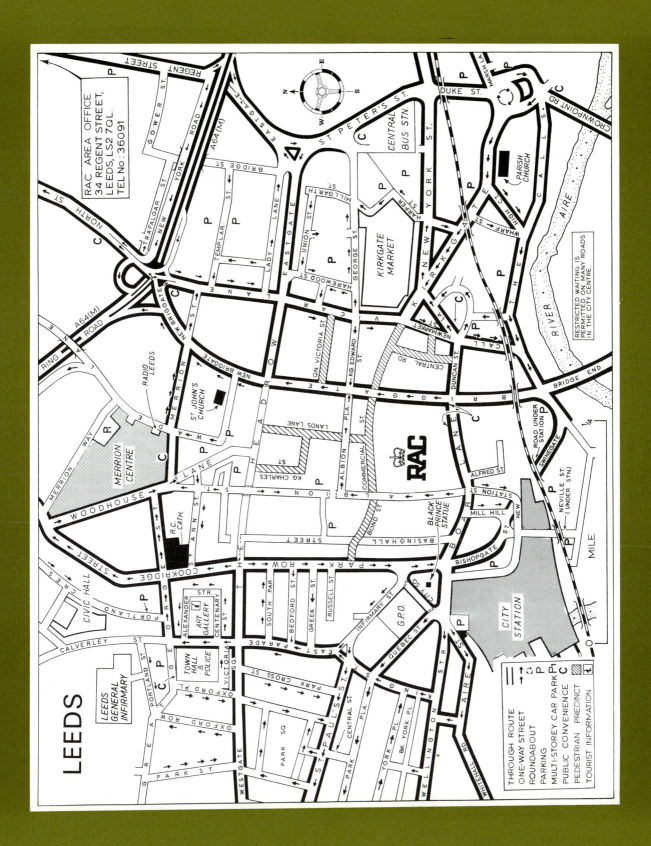

LEEDS

RAC AREA OFFICE
34 REGENT STREET,
LEEDS, LS2 7QL.
TEL No: 36091

RESTRICTED WAITING IS
PERMITTED ON MANY ROADS
IN THE CITY CENTRE.

LEEDS
GENERAL
INFIRMARY

MERRION
CENTRE

RADIO
LEEDS

ST. JOHN'S
CHURCH

R.C.
CATH.

CIVIC HALL

TOWN HALL
& POLICE

ART
GALLERY

KIRKGATE
MARKET

PARISH
CHURCH

CENTRAL
BUS STN.

RAC

BLACK
PRINCE
STATUE

G.P.O.

CITY
STATION

RIVER AIRE

THROUGH ROUTE
ONE-WAY STREET
ROUNDABOUT
PARKING
MULTI-STOREY CAR PARK
PUBLIC CONVENIENCE
PEDESTRIAN PRECINCT
TOURIST INFORMATION

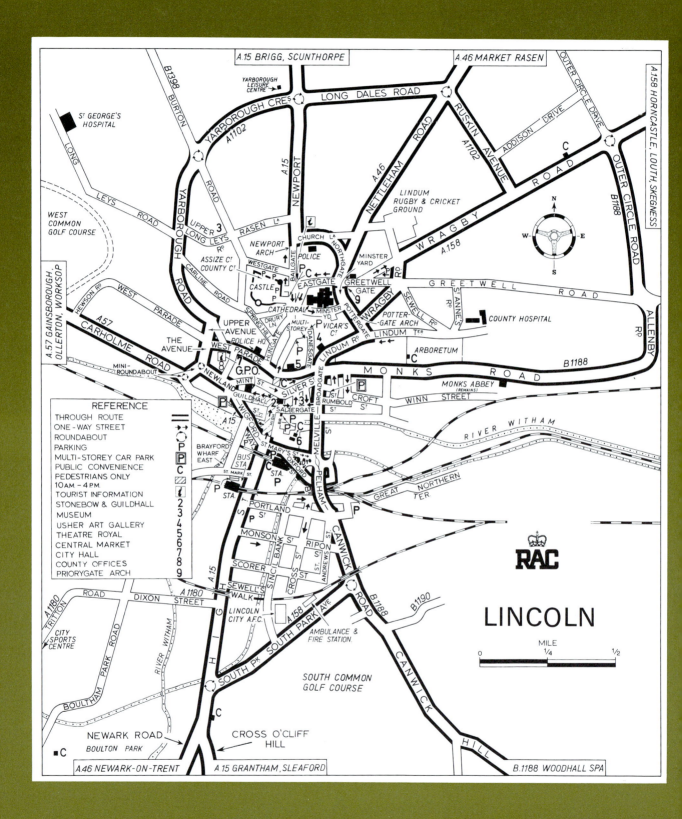

LINCOLN

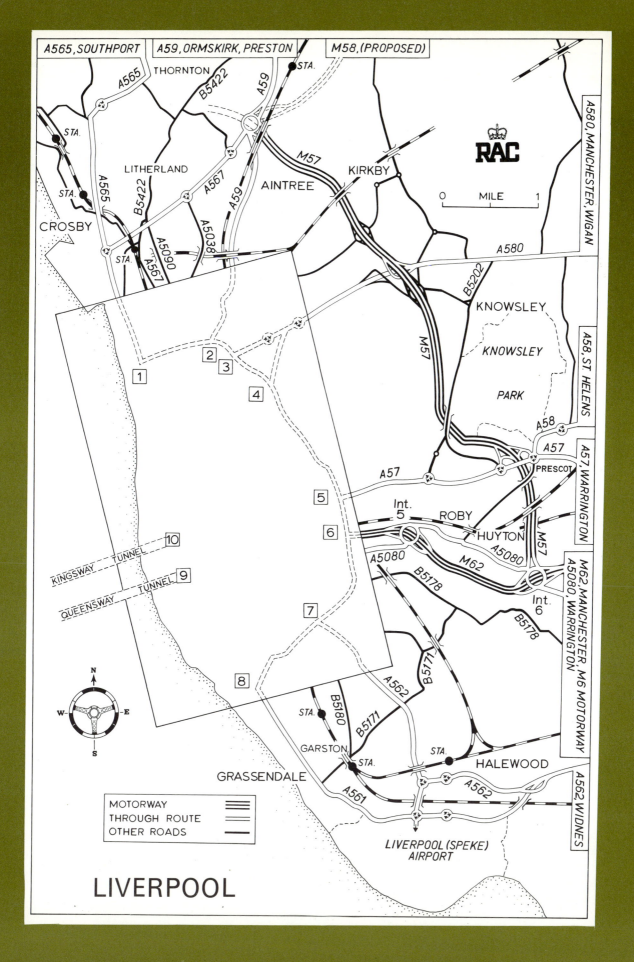

LIVERPOOL

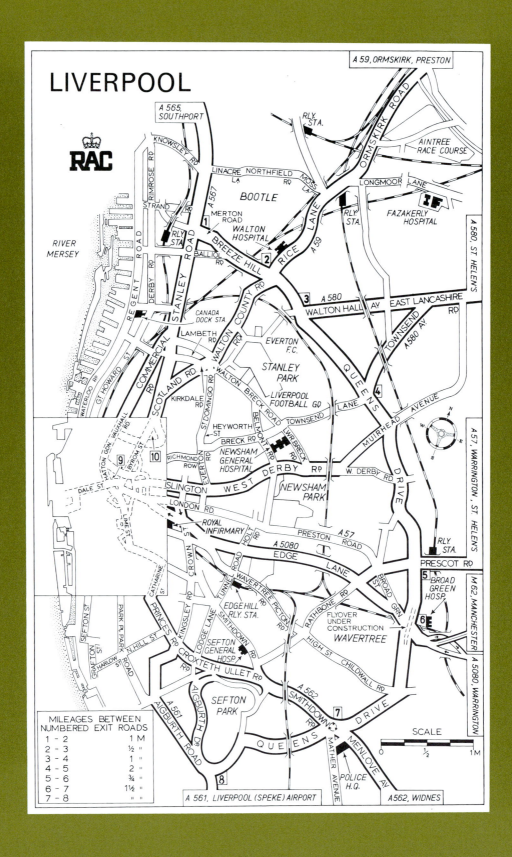

LIVERPOOL

RAC

MILEAGES BETWEEN
NUMBERED EXIT ROADS

1 - 2	1 M
2 - 3	½ "
3 - 4	1 "
4 - 5	2 "
5 - 6	¾ "
6 - 7	1½ "
7 - 8	" "

SCALE

0   ½   1M

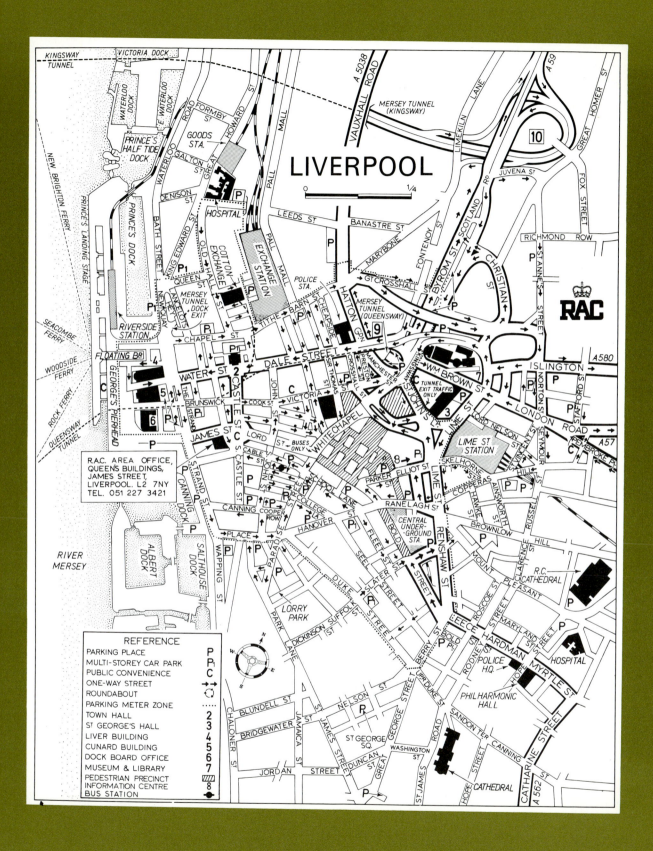

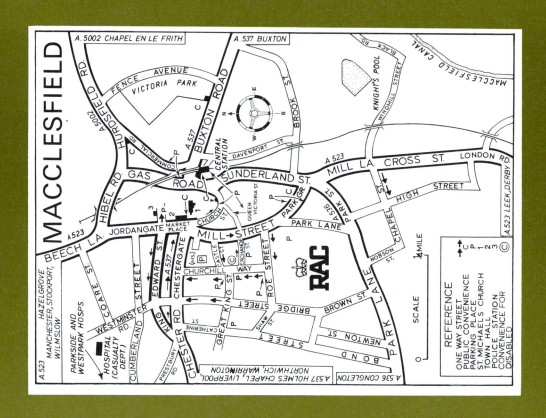

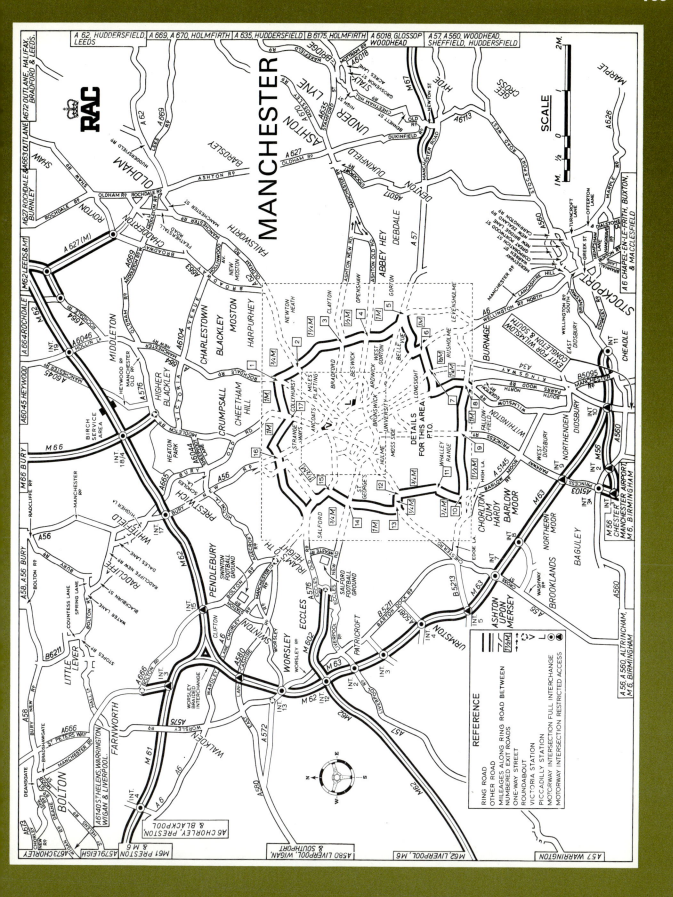

MANCHESTER

A 62, OLDHAM, M 62, LEEDS

ASHTON-UNDER-LYNE
A662   A635

A 57, HYDE & SHEFFIELD

SCALE

1 MILE.

FOR DETAILS
OF THIS AREA
SEE BELOW

REFERENCE

P	PARKING PLACE
⟷	ONE-WAY STREET
⟳	ROUNDABOUT
C	PUBLIC CONVENIENCE
T	G.P.O. (SPRING GARDENS)
M	TOWN HALL (ALBERT SQUARE)
X	CATHEDRAL

RAC AREA OFFICE,
135 DICKENSON ROAD,
MANCHESTER.
M14 5HU.
TEL. 061. 224. 3201

RAC

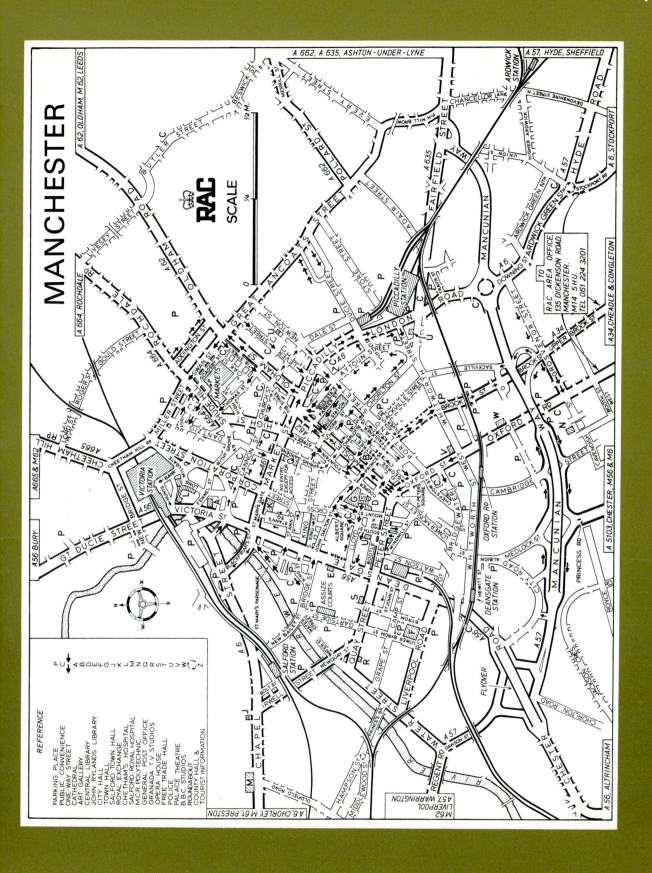

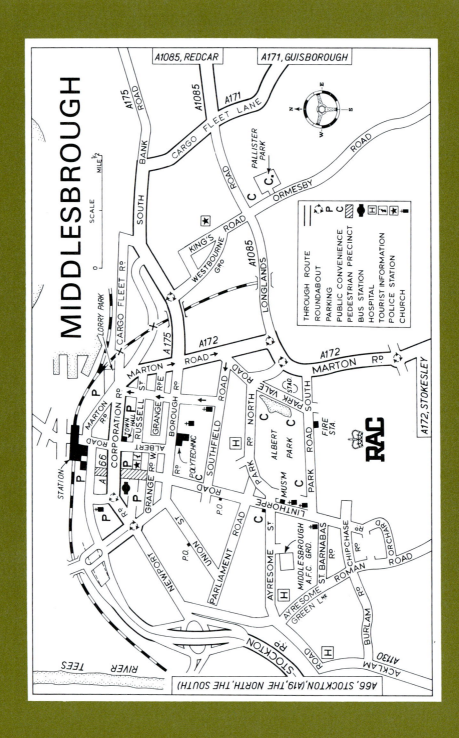

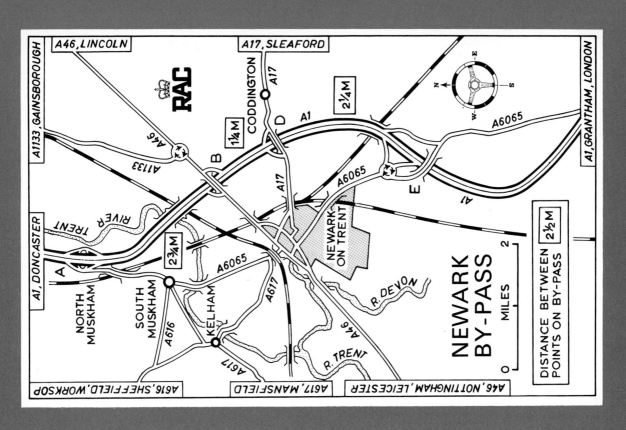

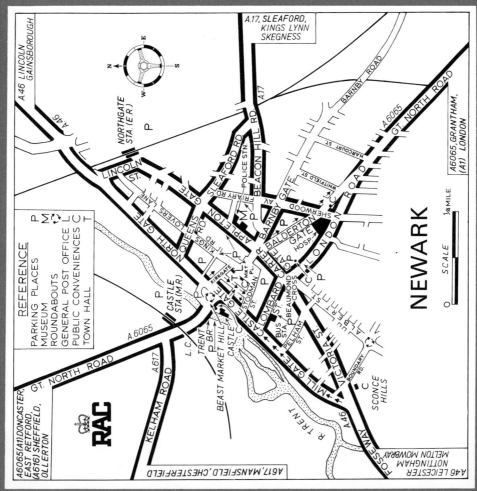

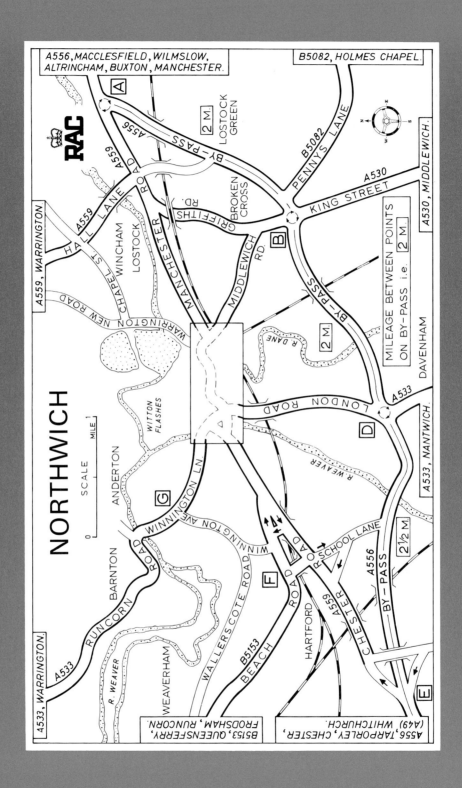

NORTHWICH

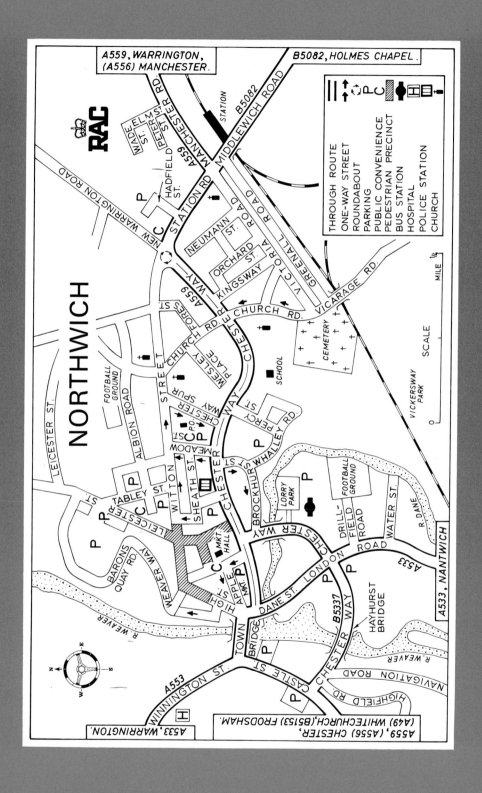

NORTHWICH

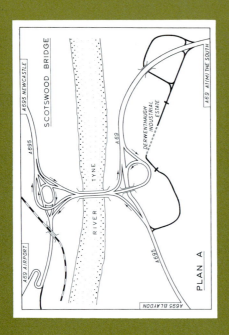

PLAN A

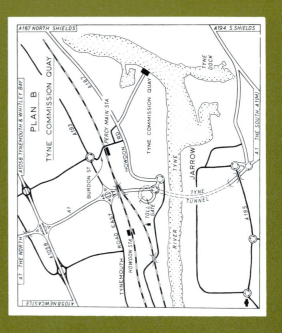

PLAN B

TYNE COMMISSION QUAY

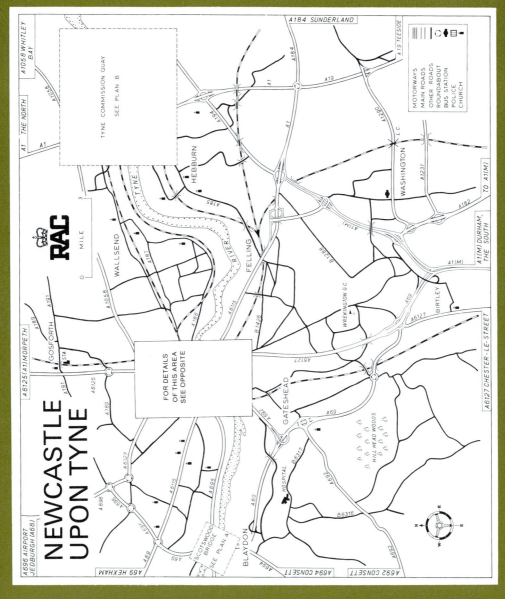

NEWCASTLE UPON TYNE

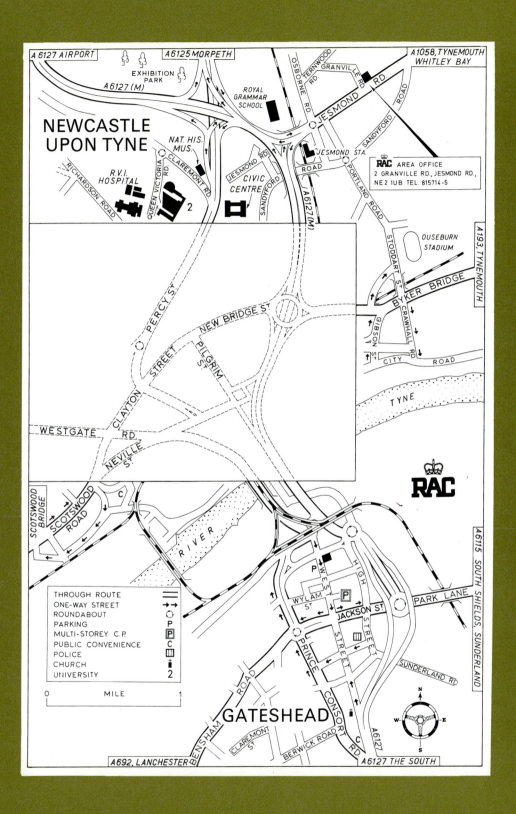

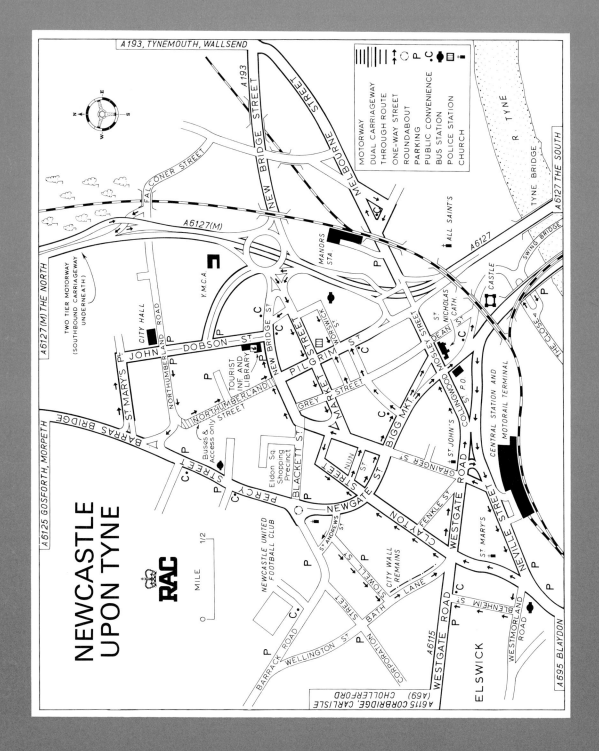

NEWCASTLE UPON TYNE

RAC

MILE

0   1/2

A6125 GOSFORTH, MORPETH

A6127(M) THE NORTH

A193, TYNEMOUTH, WALLSEND

TWO TIER MOTORWAY
(SOUTHBOUND CARRIAGEWAY
UNDERNEATH)

A6127(M)

A193

NEW BRIDGE STREET

MELBOURNE STREET

FALCONER STREET

BARRAS BRIDGE

ST MARY'S PL

JOHN   DOBSON   ST

CITY HALL

NORTHUMBERLAND   ROAD

Y.M.C.A.

MANORS STA

† ALL SAINT'S

A6127

TYNE BRIDGE

A6127 THE SOUTH

R. TYNE

SWING BRIDGE

THE CLOSE

CASTLE

ST NICHOLAS CATH.

ST

DEAN ST

MOSLEY STREET

COLLINGWOOD ST

P.O.

TOURIST
INF AND
LIBRARY

NEW BRIDGE ST

PILGRIM STREET

MOSWICK ST

GREY   ST

MARKET   STREET

BIGG MKT.

GREY   ST

NORTHUMBERLAND   STREET

Buses &
Access only

PERCY   STREET

Eldon Sq
Shopping
Precinct

BLACKETT   ST

NUN   ST

GRAINGER ST

ST JOHN'S

ST

CENTRAL STATION AND
MOTORAIL TERMINAL

NEWGATE   ST

CLAYTON   ST

FENKLE ST

WESTGATE   ROAD

ST MARY'S

NEVILLE   STREET

ST ANDREWS   ST

STOWELL   ST

BATH   LANE

CITY WALL
REMAINS

CORPORATION   STREET

WELLINGTON   ST

BARRACK   ROAD

NEWCASTLE UNITED
FOOTBALL CLUB

BLENHEIM   ST

WESTMORLAND   ROAD

WESTGATE   ROAD

A6115

ELSWICK

A695 BLAYDON

A6115 CORBRIDGE, CARLISLE
CHOLLERFORD (A69)

Legend

MOTORWAY
DUAL CARRIAGEWAY
THROUGH ROUTE
ONE-WAY STREET
ROUNDABOUT
PARKING
PUBLIC CONVENIENCE
BUS STATION
POLICE STATION
CHURCH

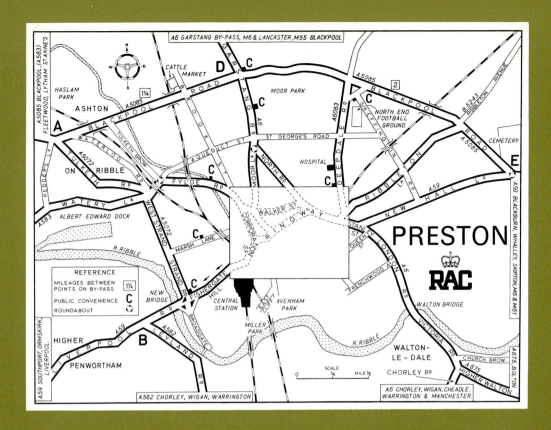

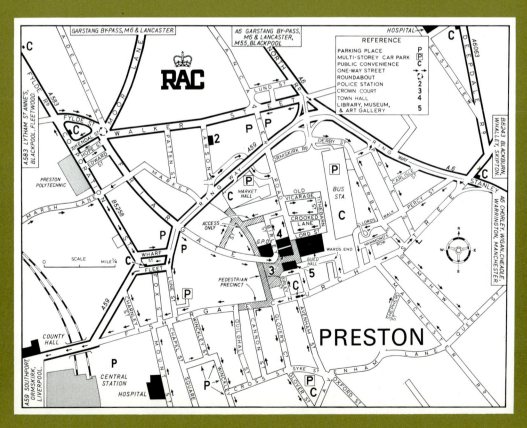

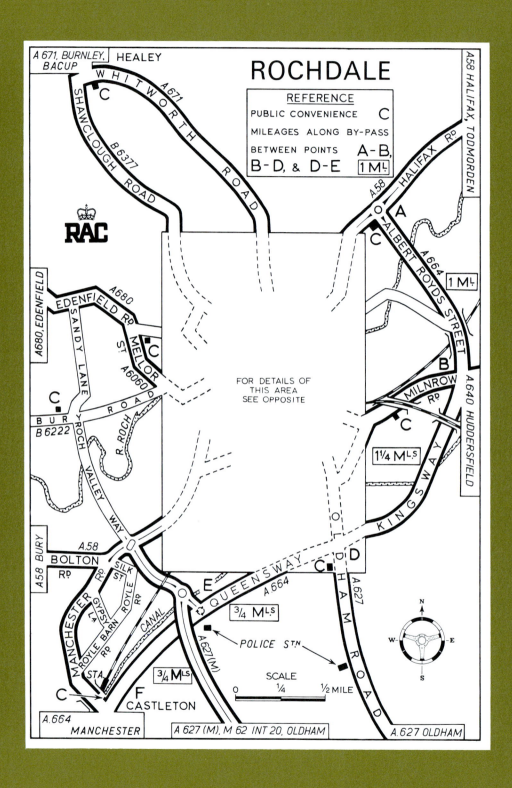

ROCHDALE

REFERENCE

PUBLIC CONVENIENCE   C

MILEAGES ALONG BY-PASS

BETWEEN POINTS   A-B,

B-D, & D-E   1 Mᴸ·

RAC

FOR DETAILS OF
THIS AREA
SEE OPPOSITE

POLICE Sᵀᴺ·

SCALE

0   ¼   ½ MILE

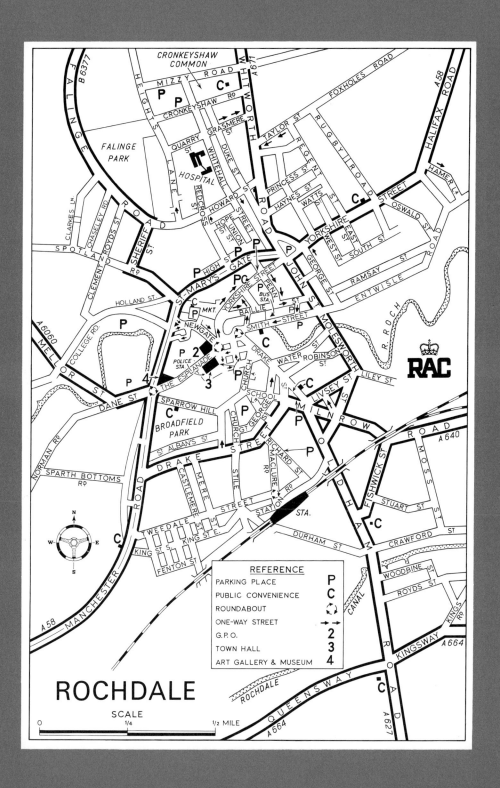

ROCHDALE

SCALE

0 — 1/4 — 1/2 MILE

REFERENCE

PARKING PLACE	P
PUBLIC CONVENIENCE	C
ROUNDABOUT	↻
ONE-WAY STREET	→
G.P.O.	2
TOWN HALL	3
ART GALLERY & MUSEUM	4

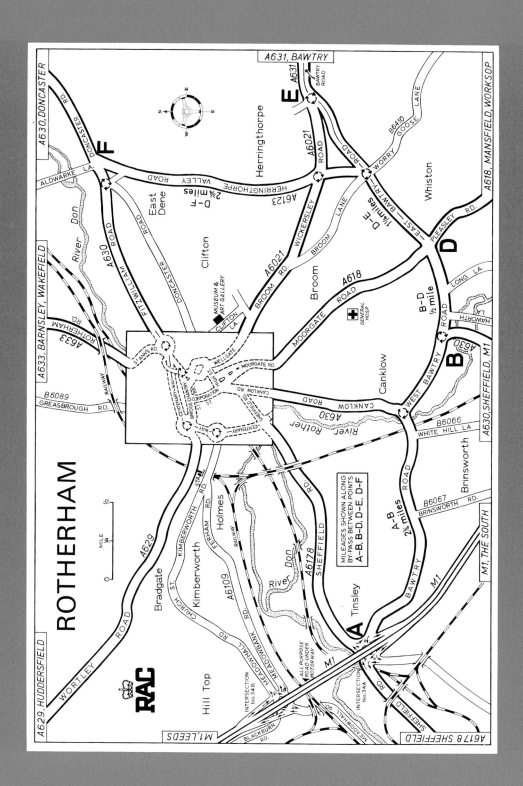

ROTHERHAM

RAC

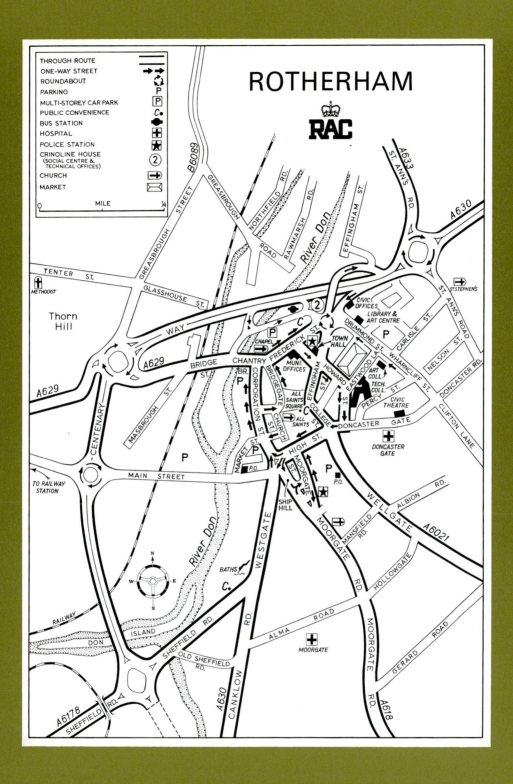

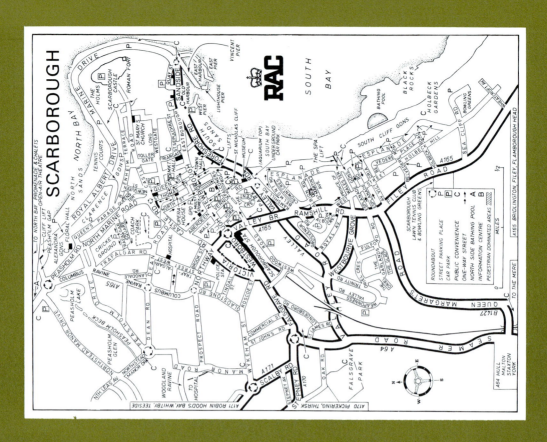

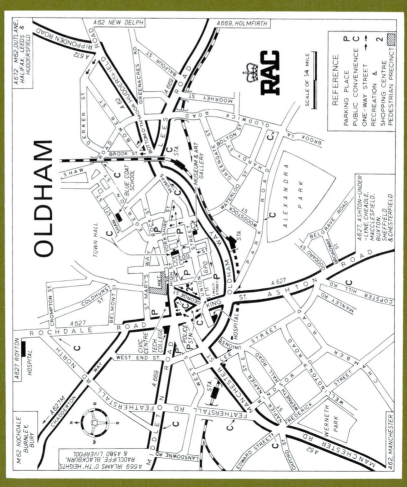

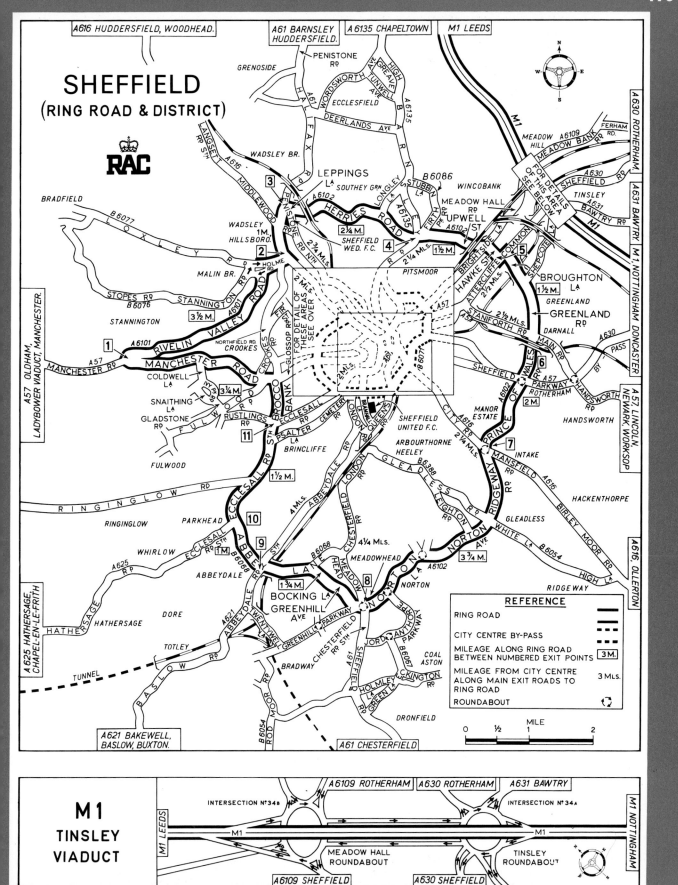

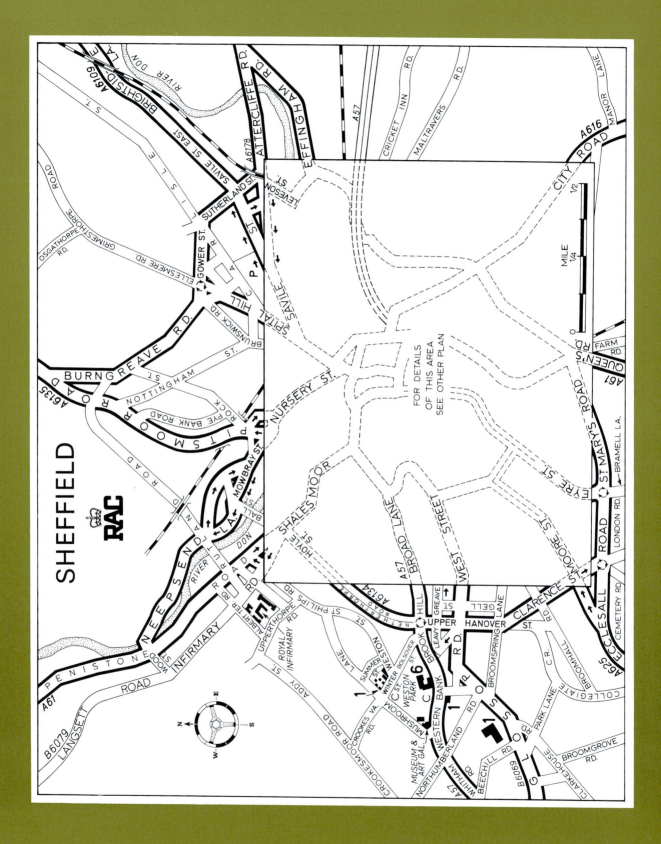

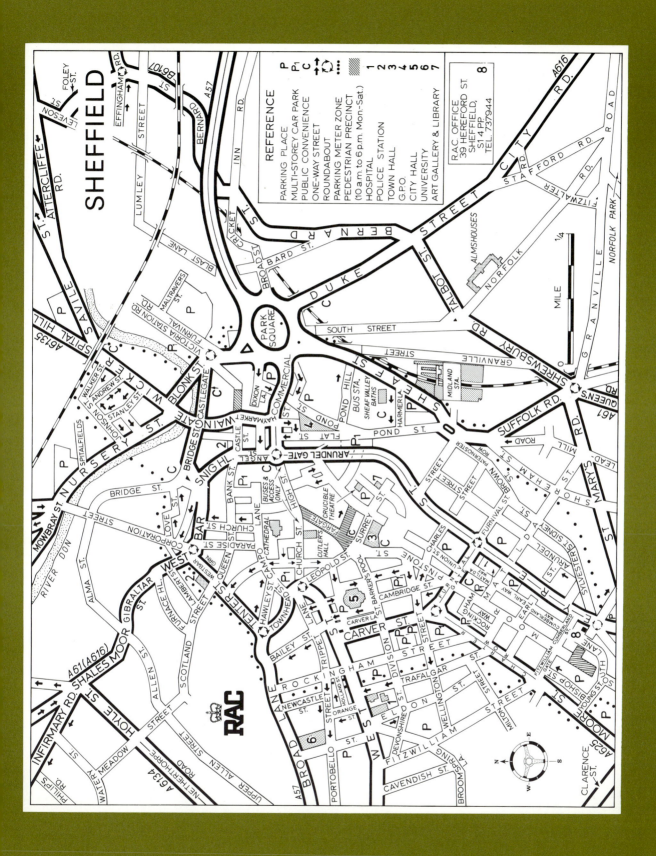

SHEFFIELD

REFERENCE

P	PARKING PLACE
P₁	MULTI-STOREY CAR PARK
C	PUBLIC CONVENIENCE
→	ONE-WAY STREET
↺	ROUNDABOUT
⋮	PARKING METER ZONE
▨	PEDESTRIAN PRECINCT (10a.m. to 6 p.m. Mon–Sat.)
1	HOSPITAL
2	POLICE STATION
3	TOWN HALL
4	G.P.O.
5	CITY HALL
6	UNIVERSITY
7	ART GALLERY & LIBRARY

8	RAC OFFICE 39 HEREFORD ST. SHEFFIELD, S14PP TEL. 737944

RAC

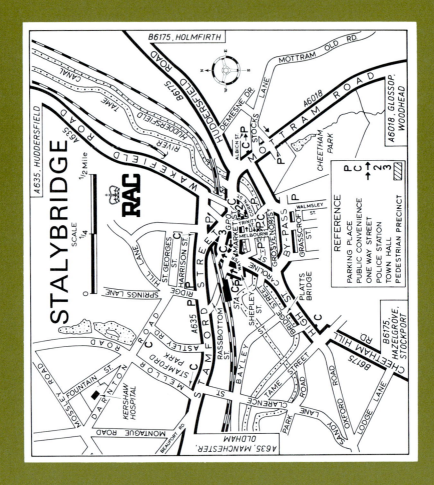

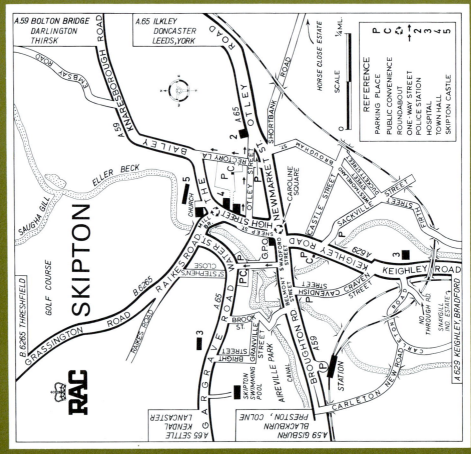

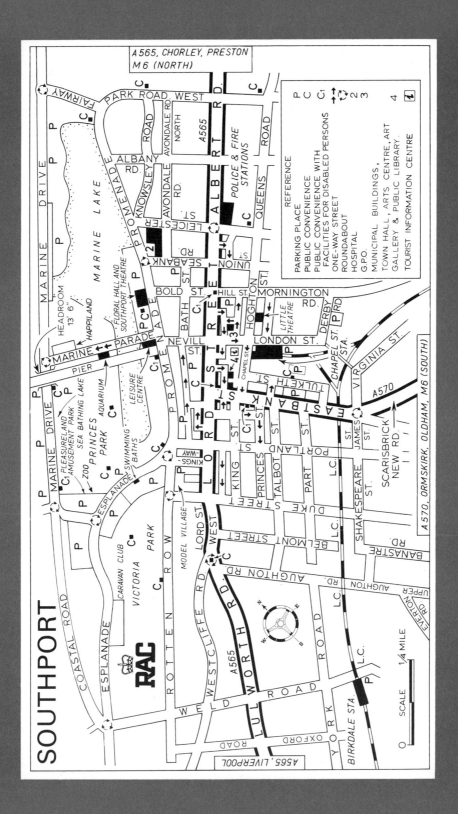

SOUTHPORT

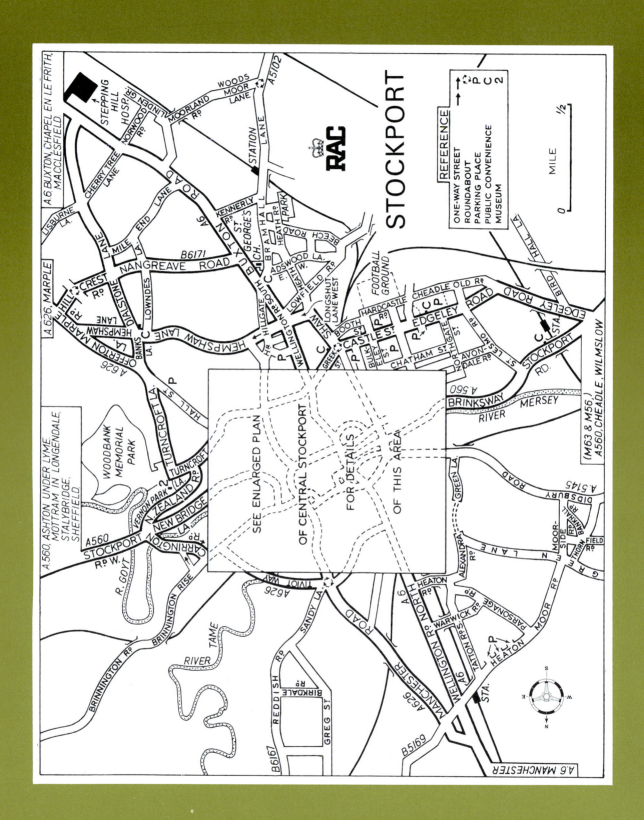

STOCKPORT

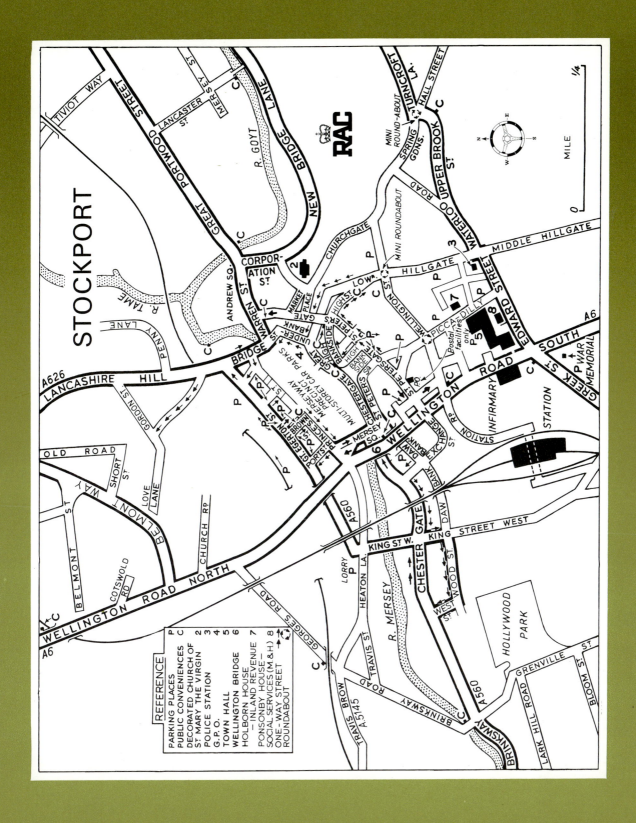

STOCKPORT

RAC

REFERENCE
PARKING PLACES .... P
PUBLIC CONVENIENCES C
DECORATED CHURCH OF
ST MARY THE VIRGIN 2
POLICE STATION 3
G.P.O. 4
TOWN HALL 5
WELLINGTON BRIDGE 6
HOLBORN HOUSE
— INLAND REVENUE 7
PONSONBY HOUSE —
SOCIAL SERVICES (M.&H.) 8
ONE-WAY STREET →
ROUNDABOUT ⟲

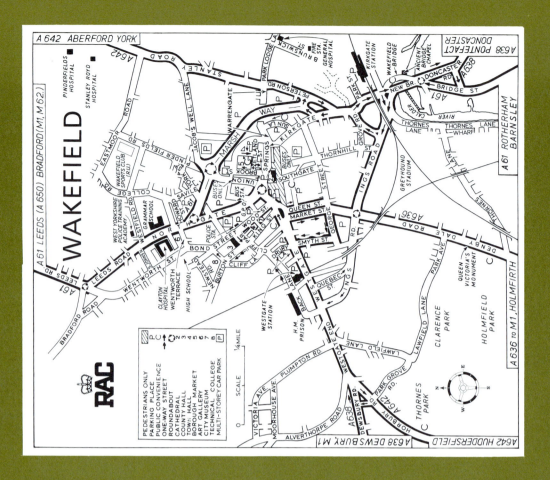

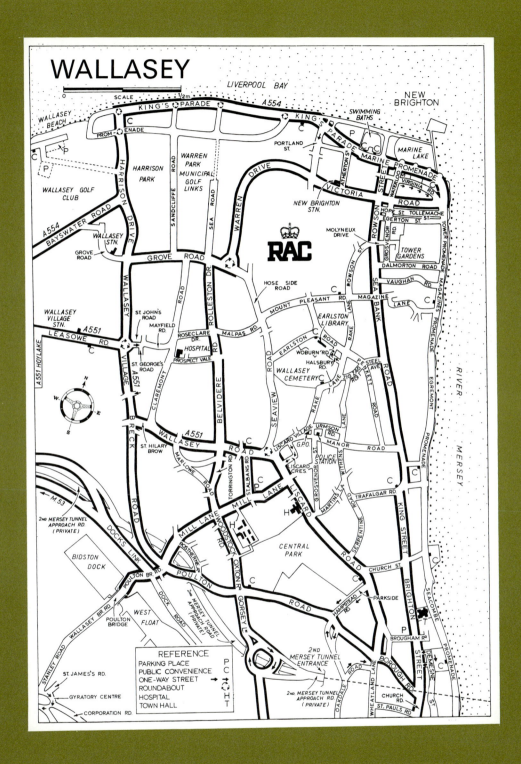

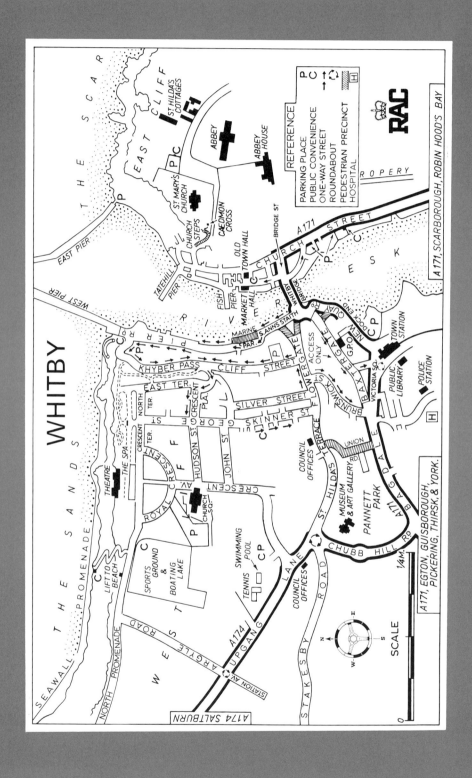

WHITBY

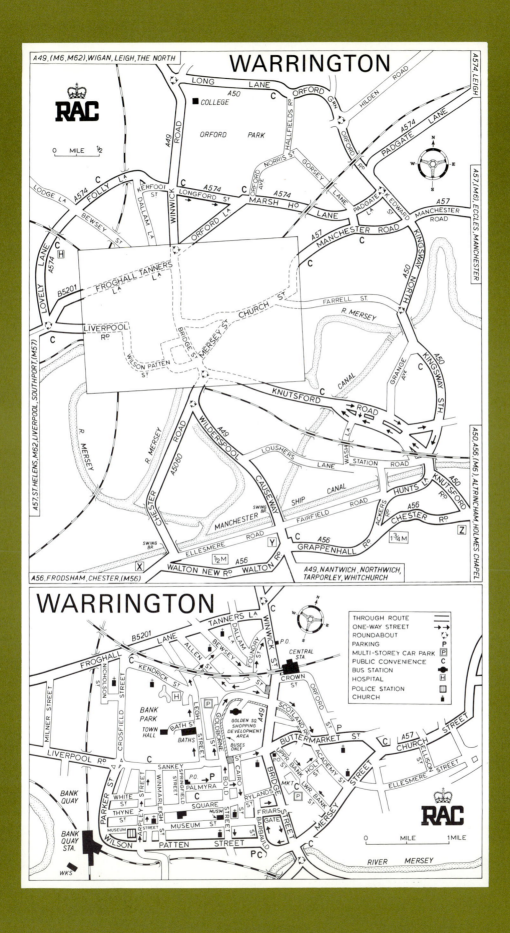

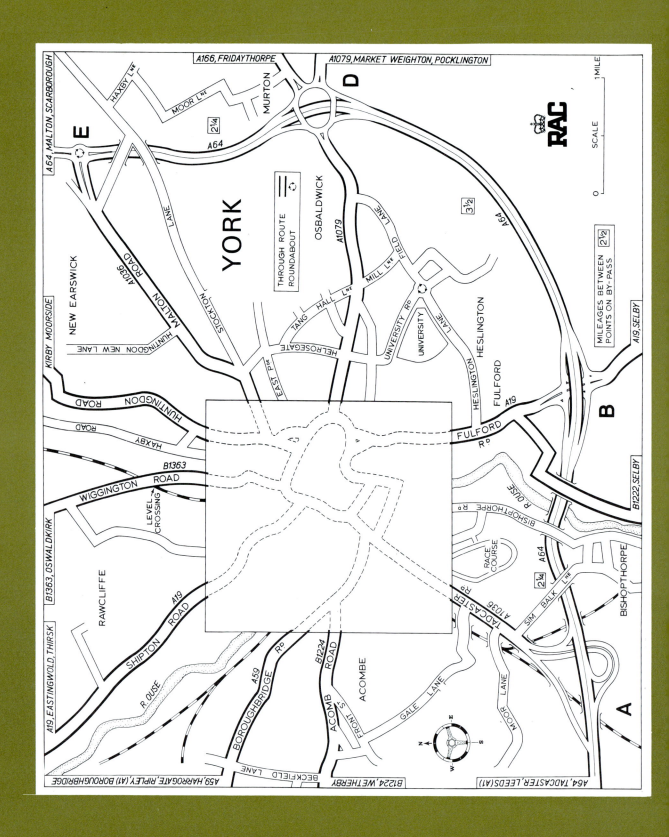

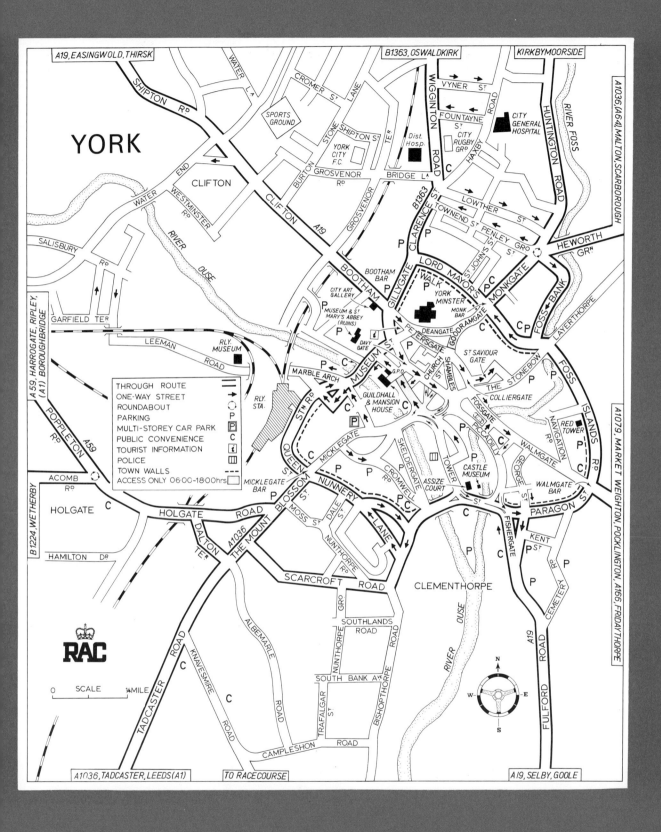

YORK

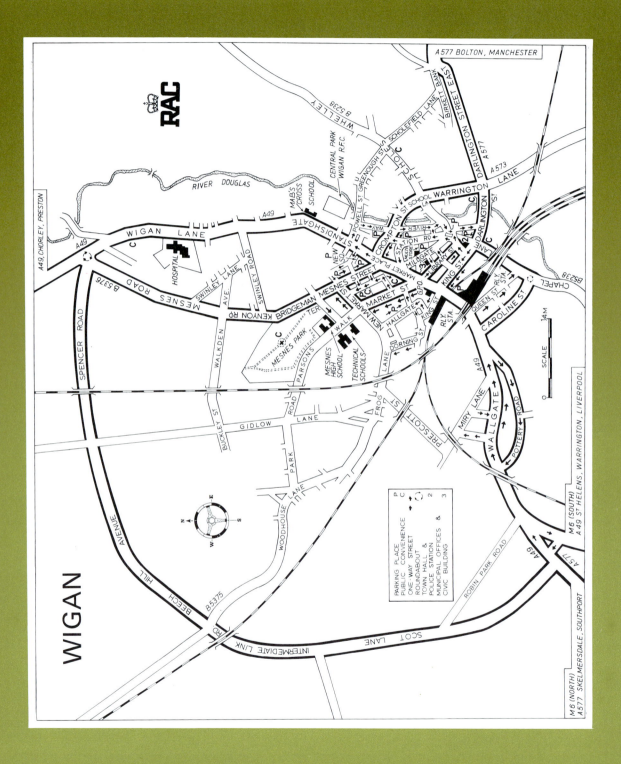

WIGAN

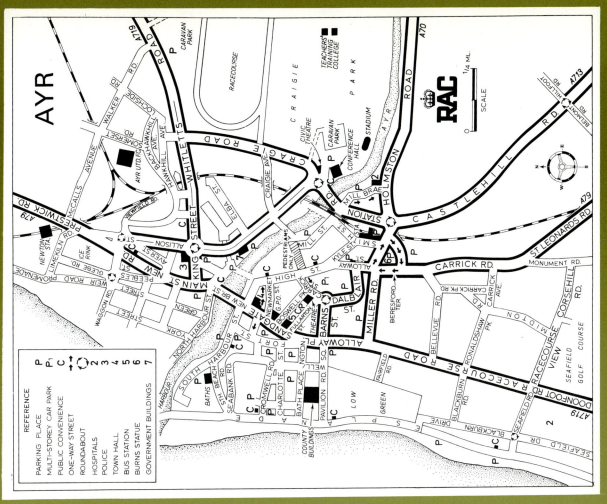

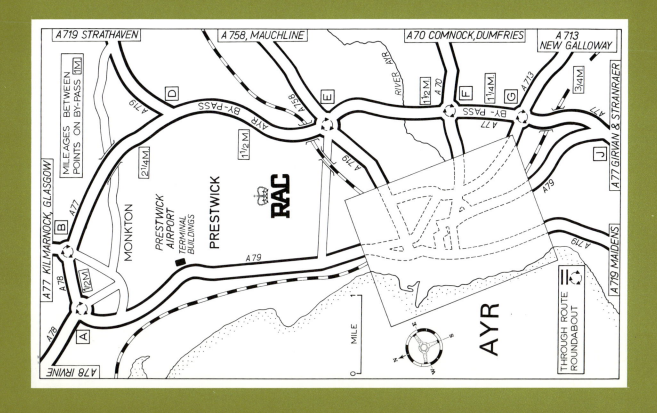

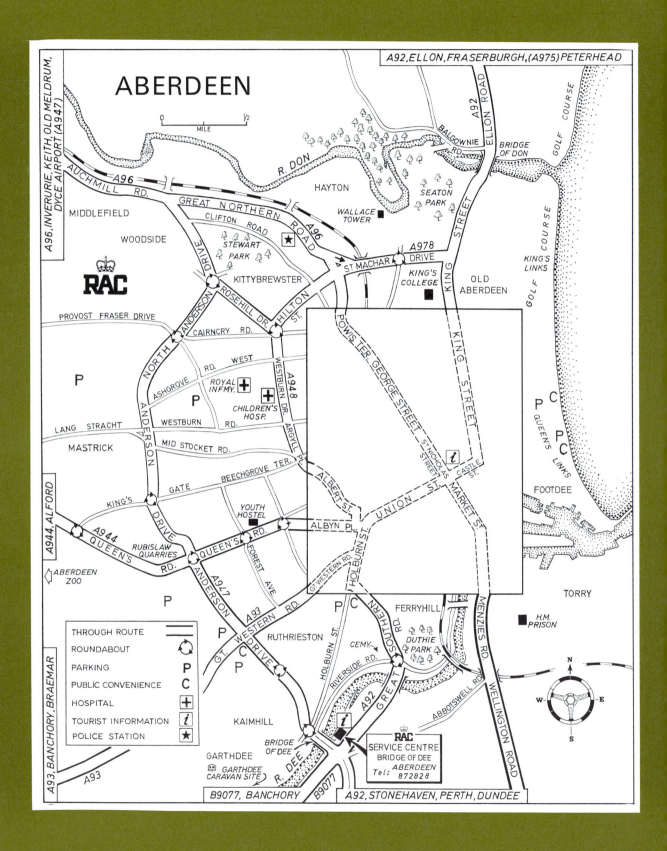

ABERDEEN

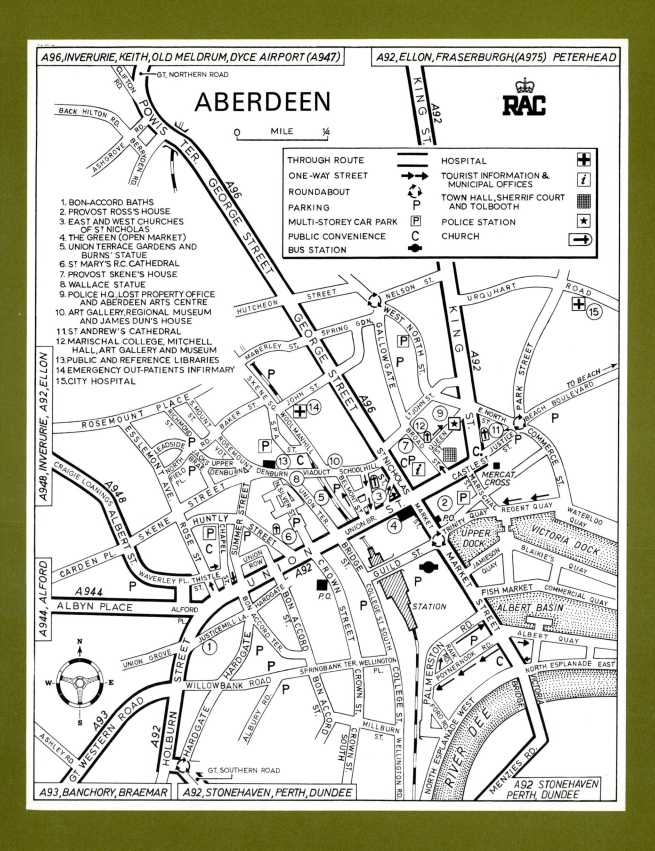

ABERDEEN

A96, INVERURIE, KEITH, OLD MELDRUM, DYCE AIRPORT (A947)

A92, ELLON, FRASERBURGH, (A975) PETERHEAD

RAC

MILE   0   ¼

1. BON-ACCORD BATHS
2. PROVOST ROSS'S HOUSE
3. EAST AND WEST CHURCHES OF S.T NICHOLAS
4. THE GREEN (OPEN MARKET)
5. UNION TERRACE GARDENS AND BURNS' STATUE
6. S.T MARY'S R.C. CATHEDRAL
7. PROVOST SKENE'S HOUSE
8. WALLACE STATUE
9. POLICE H.Q., LOST PROPERTY OFFICE AND ABERDEEN ARTS CENTRE
10. ART GALLERY, REGIONAL MUSEUM AND JAMES DUN'S HOUSE
11. S.T ANDREW'S CATHEDRAL
12. MARISCHAL COLLEGE, MITCHELL HALL, ART GALLERY AND MUSEUM
13. PUBLIC AND REFERENCE LIBRARIES
14. EMERGENCY OUT-PATIENTS INFIRMARY
15. CITY HOSPITAL

THROUGH ROUTE
ONE-WAY STREET
ROUNDABOUT
PARKING
MULTI-STOREY CAR PARK
PUBLIC CONVENIENCE
BUS STATION

HOSPITAL
TOURIST INFORMATION & MUNICIPAL OFFICES
TOWN HALL, SHERRIF COURT AND TOLBOOTH
POLICE STATION
CHURCH

A93, BANCHORY, BRAEMAR

A92, STONEHAVEN, PERTH, DUNDEE

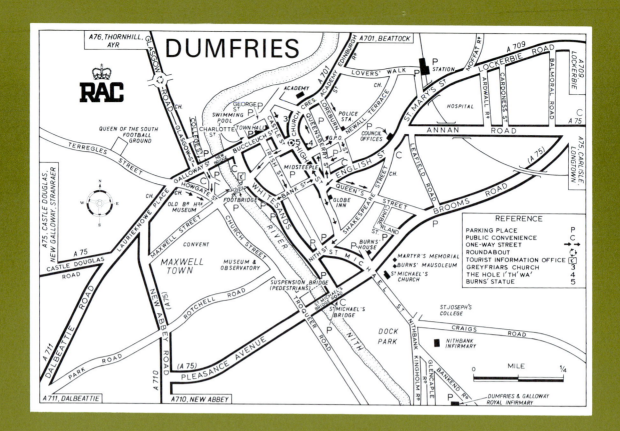

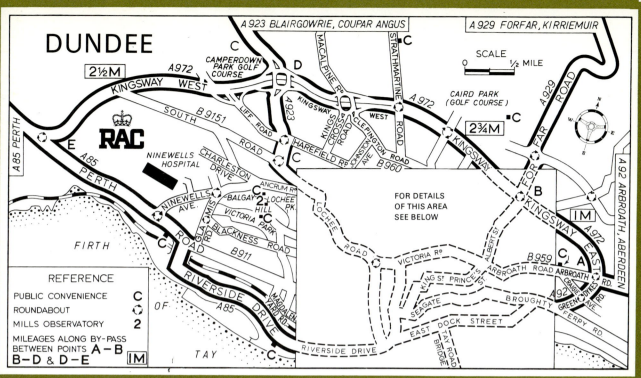

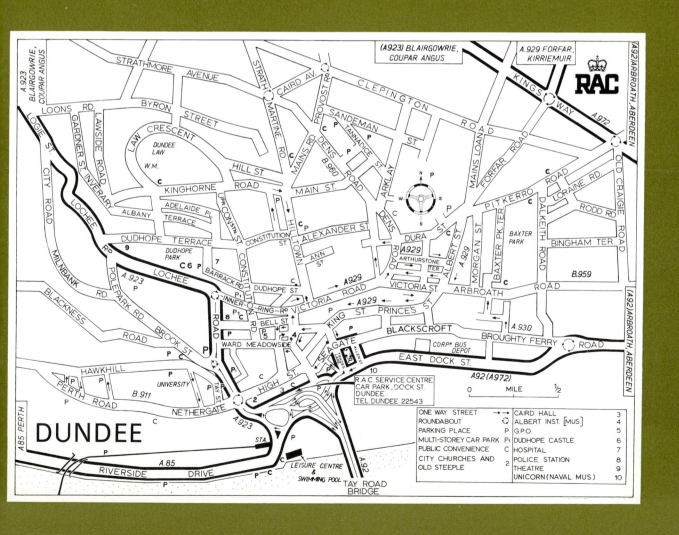

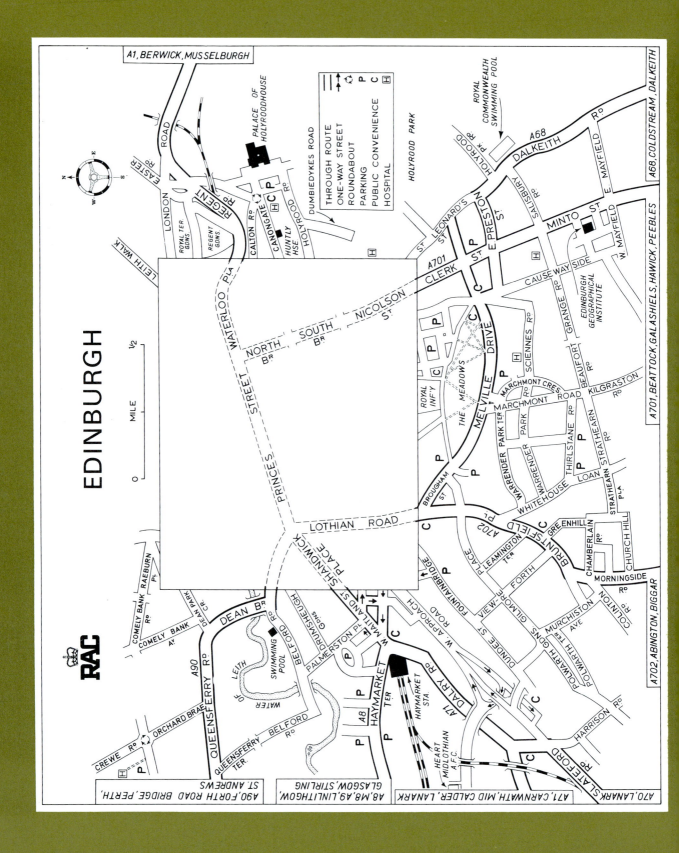

EDINBURGH

RAC

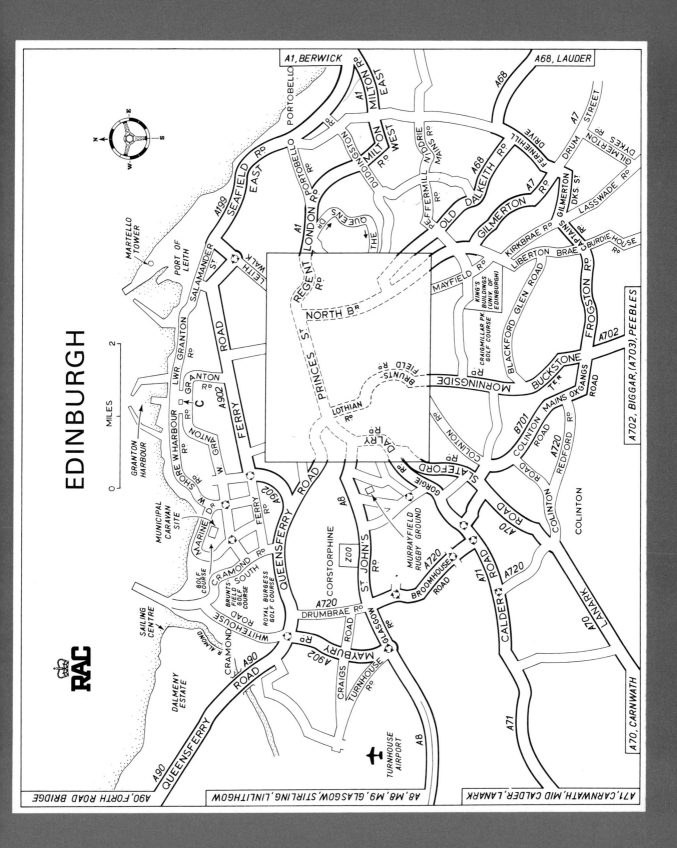

EDINBURGH

RAC

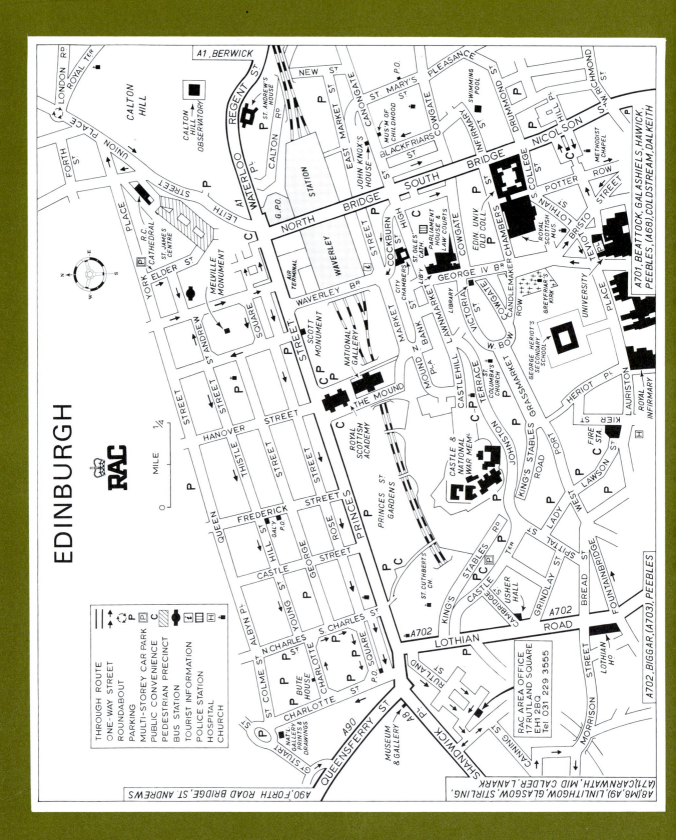

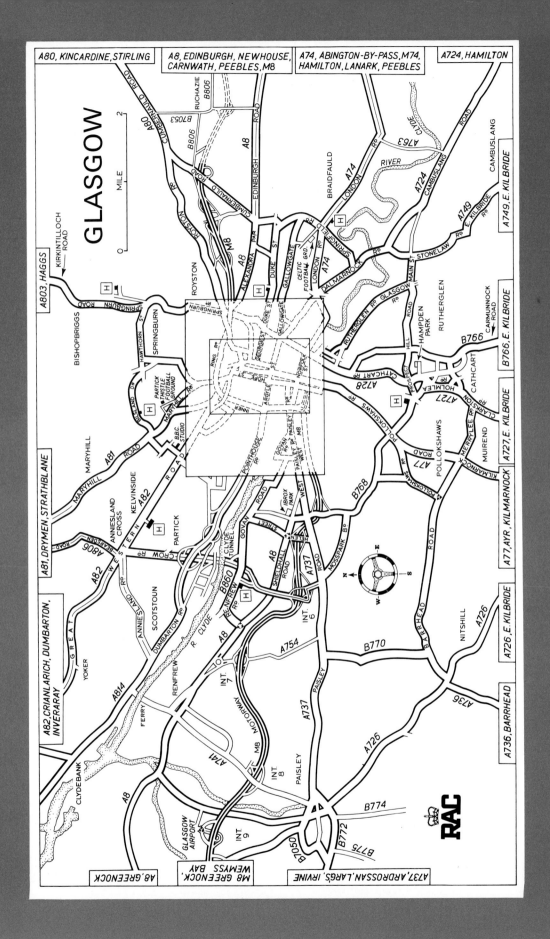

GLASGOW

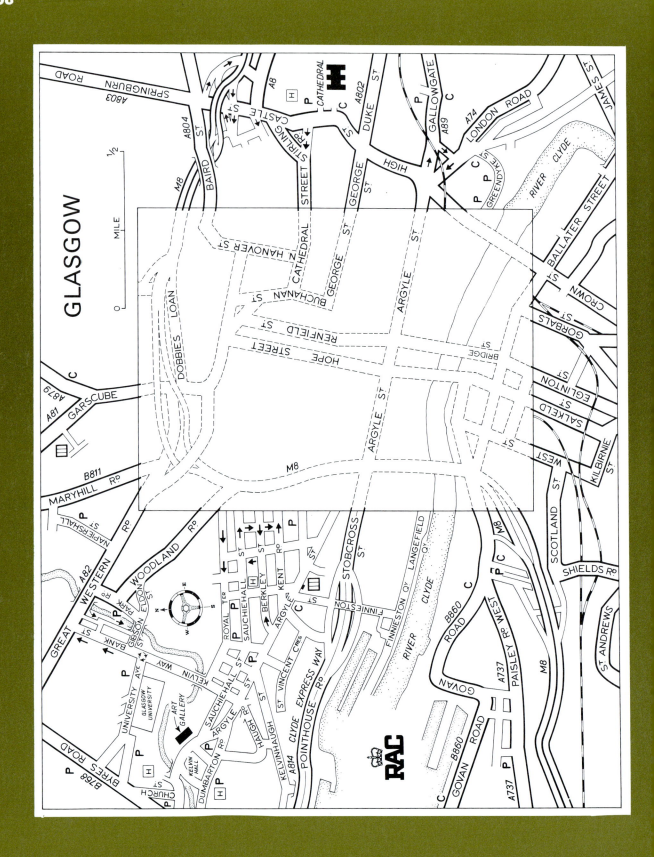

GLASGOW

GLASGOW

RAC

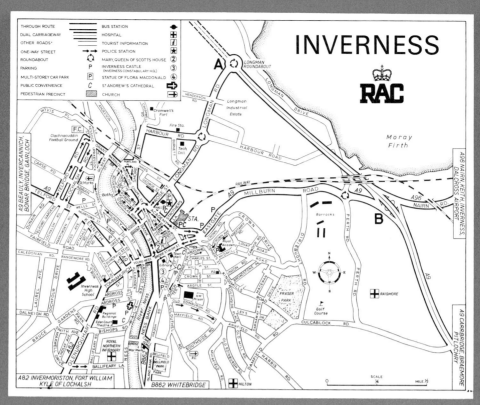

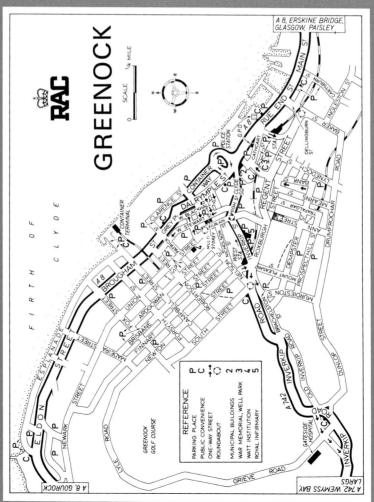

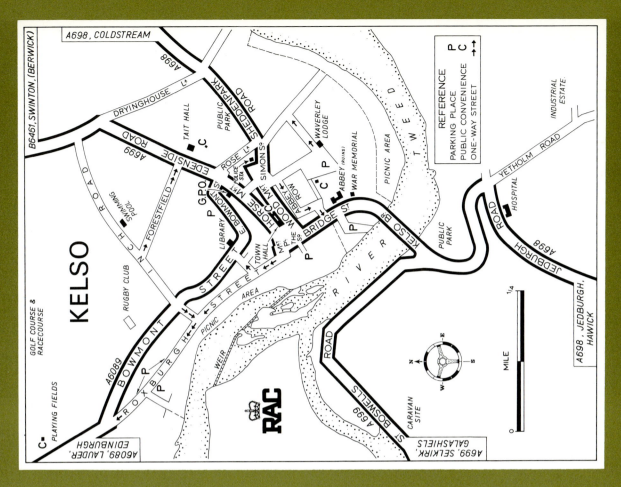

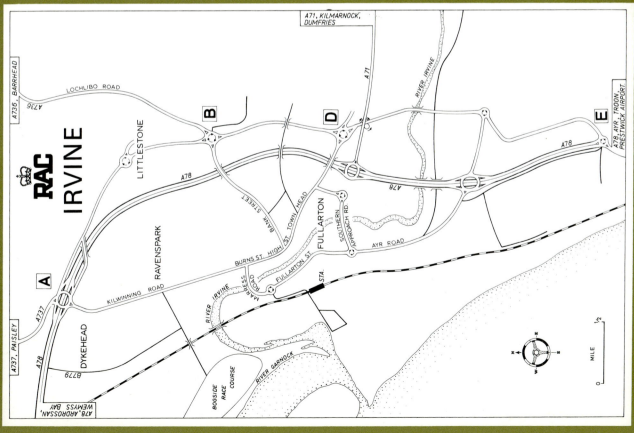

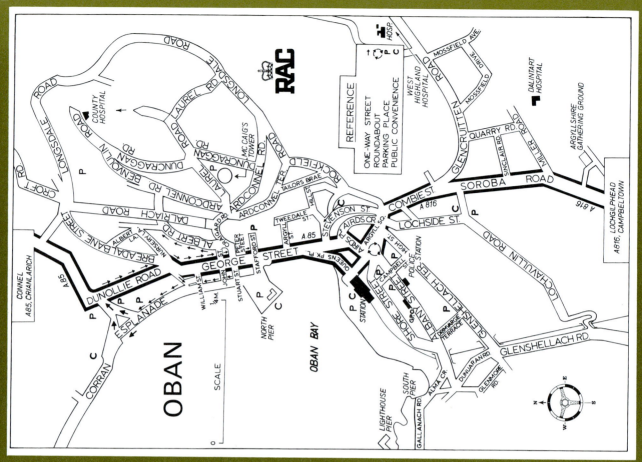

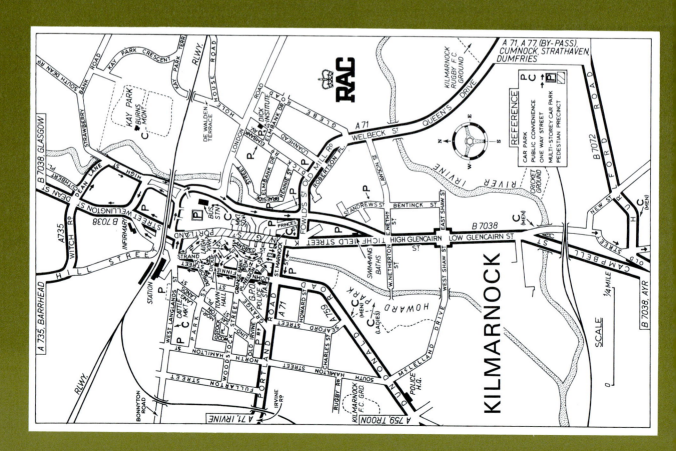

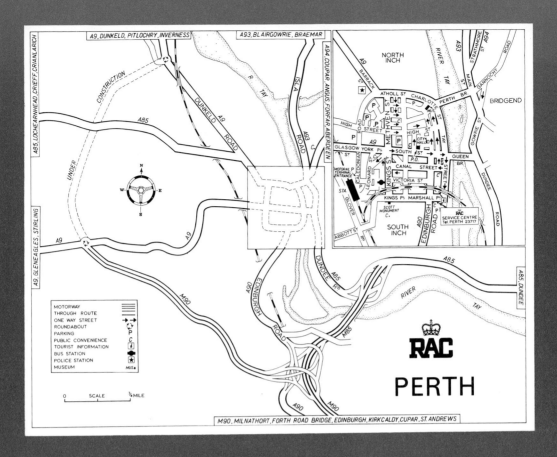

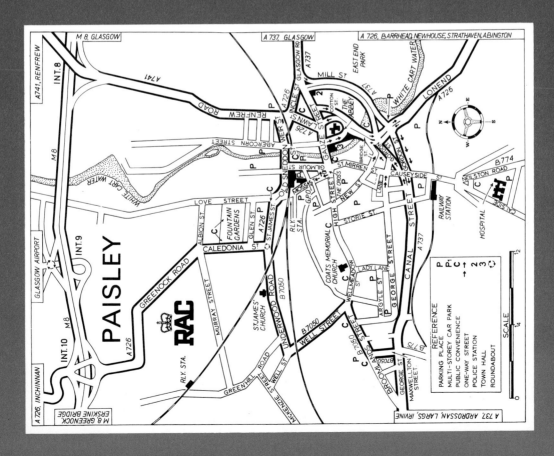

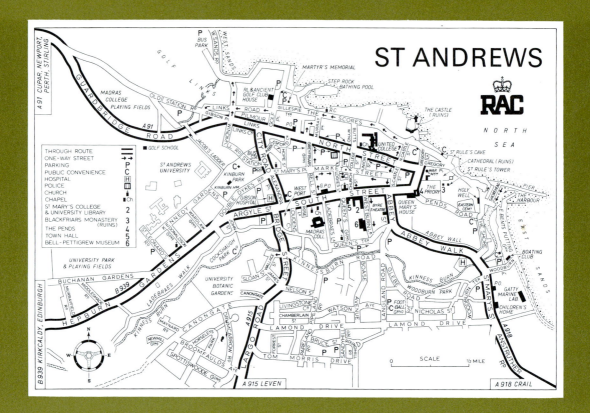

ST ANDREWS

RAC

REFERENCE	
THROUGH ROUTE	
ONE-WAY STREET	
PARKING	P
PUBLIC CONVENIENCE	C
HOSPITAL	H
POLICE	
CHURCH	
CHAPEL	Ch
St MARY'S COLLEGE & UNIVERSITY LIBRARY	2
BLACKFRIARS MONASTERY (RUINS)	3
THE PENDS	4
TOWN HALL	5
BELL-PETTIGREW MUSEUM	6

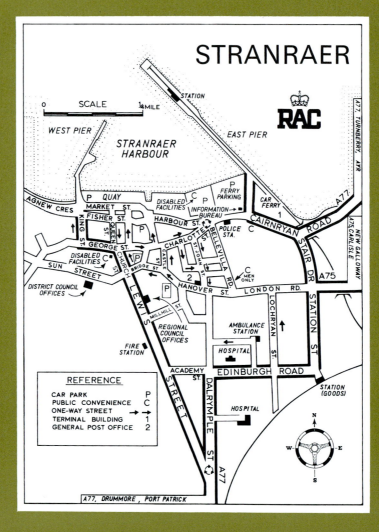

STRANRAER

RAC

REFERENCE	
CAR PARK	P
PUBLIC CONVENIENCE	C
ONE-WAY STREET	→
TERMINAL BUILDING	1
GENERAL POST OFFICE	2

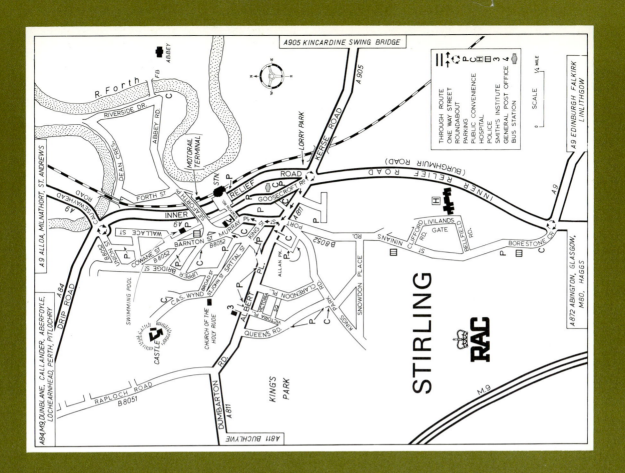

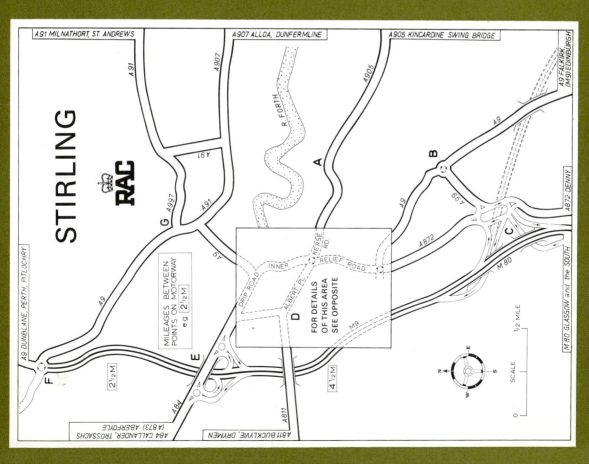

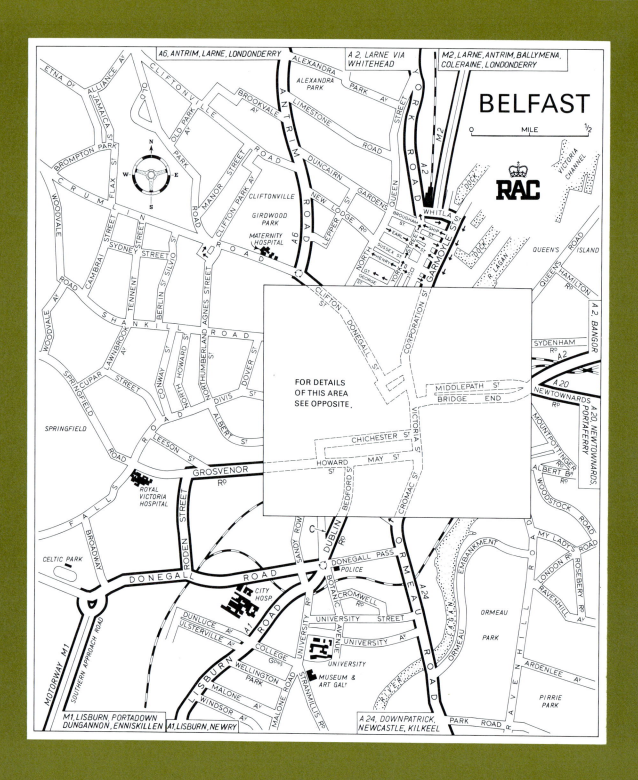

BELFAST

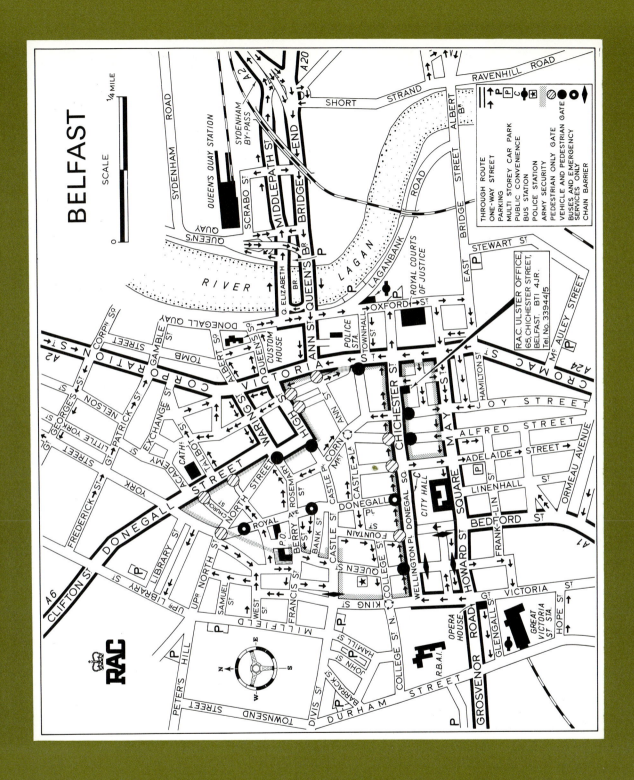

BELFAST

SCALE

¼ MILE

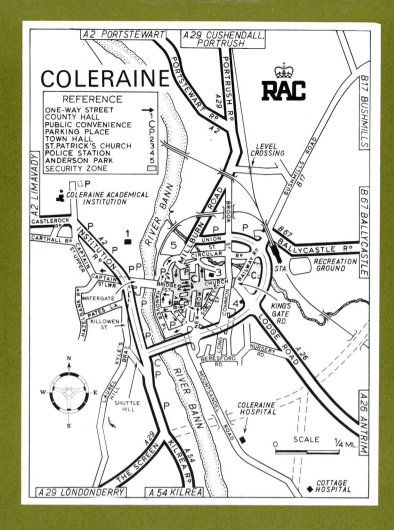

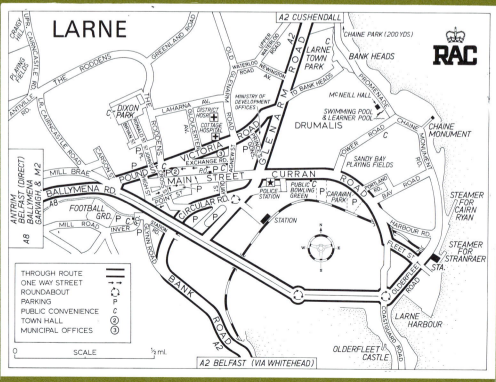